# NEVER
## SAY NO!

# NEVER SAY NO!

The Complete Program
for a Happier and
More Cooperative Dog

## DR. ROGER MUGFORD

Originally published in Great Britain
as *Dog Training the Mugford Way*

*A Perigee Book*

A Perigee Book
published by
The Berkley Publishing Group
200 Madison Avenue
New York, NY 10016

First American Edition: December 1994

The majority of photographs in this book were
specially taken by Len Cross; others are from
the author's collection. The line
illustrations are from *Just Dogs*, published by
Country Life Books in 1933.

Library of Congress Cataloging-in-Publication Data

Mugford, Roger.
    Never say no! : the complete program for a happier and
more cooperative dog / Roger Mugford.
    p.  cm.
    Includes bibliographical references and index.
    ISBN 0-399-51884-3 (alk. paper)
    1. Dogs—Training. 2. Dogs—Behavior. I. Title.
SF431.M86  1994            93-32929 CIP
636.7'0887—dc20

Printed in the United States of America

2   3   4   5   6   7   8   9   10

This book is printed on acid-free paper.

# CONTENTS

# ACKNOWLEDGMENTS

The greatest joy of my work with animals is always in their people, because dog owners are definitely among the most cheerful, sensitive and caring folk to be found anywhere. This book comes from twenty years of listening, watching and, I hope, helping these wonderful people I can be proud to call friends. To my patients and their owners, thank you, and especially thanks to those on whose behavior I was unable to work the changes that were desired and deserved. Those failures were my best instructors.

Science is a community which shares its knowledge freely, and I have been a lucky student to have had good teachers to follow. I am especially indebted to the late Dr. Norman Nowell and Professor Morley Kare of the Universities of Hull and Pennsylvania respectively. That I went on to study dogs rather than mice or chimpanzees is due to the trust and good judgment of Professor Ronald Anderson at the University of Liverpool Veterinary Faculty, who gave me my first job at the Waltham Centre for Pet Nutrition. Another fellow member of the June 3rd birthday club to whom I am extremely grateful is Devon vet and author John Bower, who was one of the first to let me loose upon his patients in the practice of behavior therapy.

Enormous thanks are due to my colleagues past and present at the

Animal Behaviour Centre, who work harder than they need for the animals we are here to help: Caroline Barnard, Kate Cogdell, Stephen Corben, Andy Denney, Karen Dunn, Penny Evans, Lis Flett, Linda Glazier, Karen Hill, Joanne Holloway, Joan Johnson, Anne McBride, Peter Neville, Cynthia Noakes, Erica Peachey, Robert Schouppe, Betsy Skinner, Nicolene Swanepoel, Claire Thatcher, Sue Williams, and especially to the most patient and loyal colleague of all, Elizabeth Crisp.

This book would most definitely have been overdue, even stillborn, without the persistent encouragement of my literary agent and friend Faith Evans, and Marion Paull at Hutchinson, who has vastly improved the original manuscript.

Finally, the lion's share of gratitude goes to my wife Vivienne and children Ruth, Emily, James and Harry, who have put up with a year of my "going to the dogs" even more than usual. Sam, my dear setter, has been the only clear winner from the writing of this book, because he can lie peacefully beneath the desk and warm my feet. Thank you, Sam!

# INTRODUCTION

Dogs are easy to train. They think like us more than you would imagine, so there is no need to treat them as inferior, dumb creatures. They are constantly watching, often trying to copy us, and the key word is "mimicry." That is why it's natural that your dog follows you around, lies beside you, howls when you sing or sits in the driver's seat of your car.

Surely, you say, training means teaching your dog to sit, stay, come and to fetch objects? Attending classes with choke chains and all that, teaching them the meaning of that word "no"? Forget it! Dogs sit because they naturally get tired, they come to us because they naturally follow, they lie down because that's the posture of sleep. To "train" these responses is unnecessary; you need never force those postures upon your pet. If you are sensitive and sensible, just wait for the puppy or dog to do these "right" behaviors, say the magic "command" word, and reward with whatever turns him on. It may be food, it may be a grooming experience, it may be a soft word or a sideways look. The approach to training I have just described has a good scientific pedigree—it is called "instrumental learning" and contrasts with the traditional method of dog training, which was rooted in the idea of compulsion, punishment and control.

My approach to training dogs works, it works fast, and fun-loving folk need not pretend to be the domineering master over a canine slave. No need to be a macho moron when indulgence and intelligence can do the job better. It is all easier if you start with a puppy, and you can't start too young. My twenty-week puppy training system is for an ideal world, but the principles of training are the same for an adult dog as for a youngster. If you adopt a secondhand, rehomed or rescued dog, of course you take on a host of question marks, but the rewards can be even greater. You will face particular challenges and you may be following the failures of others. Wait, watch and think before you act, because to do nothing is always better than to do the wrong thing.

There are problems that every dog, like every person, presents. It may be pulling on the leash, jumping up, barking at squirrels, excavating your garden, or being horrendous in the car. This is part of my craft and profession of animal behavior therapy, to which the final third of this book is devoted. It is certainly not necessary to put up with a problem pet when his behavior can so easily be modified.

I am in favor of being soft and sentimental about dogs, but I do not favor them running amok and irritating or endangering others. These are compatible objectives because we live in a world where people need all of the love that is available, yet the world is increasingly dangerous for dogs and sometimes attitudes can be hostile.

This book is also about the pursuit of distinctiveness, of letting the personal character of your dog develop. Who wants a canine clone that conforms precisely to all the standard Woodhouse ways? Modern breeds cover such a fantastic variety of shapes and personalities that they can easily satisfy the human craving for distinctiveness. Training need not smother these individual differences.

All over the world, stringent laws are being introduced that regulate dog ownership, where dogs may go and what they can do. In part, this arises from hysteria about feces, sometimes justified fear of attacks by dogs, and, perhaps most fundamental of all, envy of the fun and love that dogs so freely give to their owners. Dogs do have to be trained, but please, don't shout, and you need never say No!

Roger Mugford
Surrey, 1992

Part One

# THE PSYCHOLOGY
# OF THE DOG

# 1

# What Every Dog Knows:
## Instincts, Senses and Language

Have you ever felt that in some uncanny way your dog knows what you are thinking? Equally, for most of the time you probably have a fair idea of your dog's likely next move. The great pleasure of living with dogs is that most of them and most of us find it easy to share the same wavelength; to think "dog" requires less effort than to think cat, horse or parrot. The philosopher Descartes, and others since, believed that the mental lives of animals and man were different and that only man experienced true consciousness. That view has been used to justify our often unkind and usually unequal treatment of animals, but now, on the verge of the twenty-first century, attitudes are changing.

Dogs are important in this evolving cultural attitude to animals because they are so obviously similar to humans in their expressions of emotions and social behavior. If family, tribe and local community are the key social groupings of people, a pack of dogs serves the same purpose. This is to cooperate, to band together so that territory can be defended, larger animals can be hunted and if sickness or adversity strikes, to care for one another.

There are only a few other animals whose sociability and altruism bear comparison with humans: wolves of course, the socially sophisticated species such as elephants, whales and dolphins, and the great apes like gorillas. It is natural for sensitive people to find pleasure in the company of these animals because they are kindred spirits: they seem to share the same emotional wavelength. It was no accident that the wolf became elevated during the course of history to the role of "man's best friend."

Anyone interested in dogs must find inspiration in the behavior of wolves, especially when they have been studied in the wild. From the pioneering work of David Mech, Eric Zimen and other ethologists, we now have a fairly comprehensive picture of the species and of how the structure and size of their packs vary in different habitats and at different seasons. Basically, when food is in short supply or times are hard, wolves come together in larger packs and there is greater emphasis upon cooperation. When food is plentiful, perhaps during the summer or when there is a seasonal rise in the availability of easy-to-catch rodents, solitary living becomes more viable, more attractive even, and there is a greater emphasis upon defense of individual territory.

Within a wolf pack, there are ritual exchanges of signals before, during and after important activities like hunting. Their precise significance may be hard for us to understand, because the speed of communication is just too fast for us to follow, and dogs rely more upon smell, less upon sight than we do. Contrary to popular belief, fighting rarely occurs between individuals of the same pack: skins of wolves which have been taken from the wild do not usually bear the scars of frequent, bloody combat. On the other hand, they will fight to defend territory against entry by strange wolves from neighboring packs, even to death.

The theory used to be that wolf packs have a rigid hierarchy or class structure within them, whereby dominance and subordinance are established during challenges between members of the pack. Unfortunately, that concept turns out to have been a statistical artifact from the work of scientists who studied wolves in captivity, leading to a sort of scientific baloney about the true nature of dog society. This hierarchical model of wolf behavior, and, by inference, of dog behavior, has misled many people into thinking that pet dogs are constantly attempting to establish an alpha, boss or top-dog status, an error that has in turn spawned the view that owners should be tough with their pets. The main losers in this mistaken model of dog behavior have been the owners: human nature mostly wants to find love in the company of dogs, but the dominance theory tells us to behave like a master who rules his slaves.

Let us call the old way of living with and training a dog the dominant way, and the philosophy expressed in this book the cooperative way. For the moment, I hope you will accept my judgment that most dogs desire to please, to manipulate and to play with us far more than they want to compete, control or brutalize. Far from proclaiming the dangers of anthropomorphism, I can comfort a non-scientifically trained reader with the latest consensus on canine behavior, from experts like Dr. Michael Fox and Dr. Randy Lockwood, which is that they think, behave and live much more like we do than most other species of animals. If you are ever in doubt about what a dog makes of a particular situation you should simply ask yourself what you would think or do.

Field studies of wolves and dogs have shown that pairs, trios and larger groups form long-term friendships or coalitions, and that they gather together for games and hunting, to defend territory and to share body warmth in sleep. You will be losing a great deal from the potential of this relationship if you just want to be the boss: much better to see your dog as a friend or partner.

I can't deny that the sensory and physiological world of the dog is different from that of man: he doesn't share our sophisticated spoken language, our unique bipedal locomotion, our relatively over-developed cerebral cortex or other specialized neurological structures and sensory systems. His is a different world, so let us begin by examining the five senses of the dog and compare them with our own.

## SMELL

More than any other sensory system, smell rules the lives of wild dogs. They need to smell to detect food—on the hoof while hunting, dead when scavenging. More important, they need to know what dangers are about, especially the movements of other dogs. What time did they pass by, what was their sex and their emotional state?

Fully one half of the cerebral cortex in the dog is given over to the sense of smell. A normally proportioned dog's nose (not one that has been squashed in like a boxer or Pekingese) is a miracle of aerodynamic engineering in which volatile chemicals are first absorbed onto moist membranes, which in turn generate chemical and electrical signals for onward transmission to the brain. It has been experimentally demonstrated that as little as one molecule of certain organic chemicals in one cubic meter of air can be detected by a dog. Dogs can smell in "stereo" by an alternation of inhalation between the right and left nostrils. By this clever system, they can "walk" up a concentration gradient of smells borne on the wind, eventually locating the source just as we humans can detect the direction of sound. Theoretically, human beings should be capable of the same stereo analysis of odor strengths, but in reality few of us have that ability. Test yourself by wearing a blindfold downwind from some strong odor source, perhaps from a factory or a silage pit. Have someone guide you around and disorientate you in relation to the source of the smell, then try to track it with your nose. You will not perform well! By contrast, dogs are able to locate a bitch in heat two miles away, relying on smell alone.

The bodies of both humans and dogs are covered in secretory structures; they are especially well developed under armpits, on the soles of feet and around the ano-genital region. The apocrine or sweat glands in man are especially important for keeping cool, whereas the dog loses about 90 percent of its heat through the remarkable series of nasal passages through which air is breathed in, exhaled by the mouth.

Sebaceous glands are structures within the skin which secrete an oily material that transports fat-soluble steroids. For many animals, sebaceous secretions provide information about sex and individual identity. Male humans and dogs share a similar mix of chemicals from metabolites of the masculine hormone testosterone, so a dog can be a good judge of what his master has been up to. Dogs are also proficient at determining the stage of estrus in females and dairy cows, even the stage of a woman's cycle, from the smell of steroids on her skin.

Within seconds of our being emotionally aroused or frightened, there is a dramatic change in the electrical conductivity of the skin as apocrine glands pour out sweat. Dried material on the skin is chemically activated with that surge of moisture, and an envelope of smells comes to surround our aroused bodies. This may be the odor of fear, of depression or of love, but be sure that we cannot hide our emotions from dogs as easily as we can from fellow humans.

Smell offers a medium for teaching dogs which has so far rarely been exploited in either the training or scientific literature. I myself investigated the odors that dogs enjoy during research for a large pet-food company. Among other things, I found that dogs prefer to eat dry food permeated with the odor of certain cooked meats and amino acid combinations, and that male dogs consistently prefer the odors of anal sacs, vaginal secretions and urine from female dogs in heat to those that are not. I also found out that most dogs are attracted to sulphury smells such as horse-hoof trimmings and to the odors of fermented products, especially the feces of herbivorous animals.

Other scientists have studied odors that repel animals, and French workers have actually devised a practical conditioning system that suppresses unwanted barking in dogs with the smell of citronella (see page 127). At our Animal Behaviour Centre we sometimes use a squirt of perfume to discourage unwanted behavior such as jumping up. I will be giving examples later of how we can exploit smell in everyday training to enhance the attractiveness of rewards and the singularity of punishments.

## TASTE

Taste is a primitive sense that we land-living animals inherit from our watery past. It is activated when chemicals dissolved in the saliva make contact with specialized taste buds or receptors on the papillae of the tongue. Your dog experiences the same four basic taste sensations as you or I: sweet, sour, bitter and salt. The function of taste is the same in dogs as in other animals: to identify nutritive foodstuffs; to avoid those which are poisonous (they usually taste bitter) and those which are spoiled by microorganisms (usually acid); and to locate the minerals which the body requires to be constantly replenished (often salty). Much of taste is a matter of pleasure seeking for sweetness, and the dog has as sweet an orientation as man.

For practical training, taste can be used as both a positive and a negative reward system. I hesitate to encourage readers to offer their pet sweets with waist-widening and tooth-rotting sugars, and it is unlikely that your dog will benefit from receiving supplementary salt. However, on the negative side, unpleasant-tasting bitter compounds may be applied to surfaces, even to the animal's own body if it is licking excessively. A number of proprietary products are available, but few are as effective as a concentrated solution of quinine or of sucrose octa-acetate. This last compound has the chemical structure of a sugar but imparts a remarkably unpleasant and long-lasting bitter taste. Both quinine and sucrose octa-acetate may be safely given to the dog in the small quantities needed to repel.

Then there is the vomeronasal organ, a tiny sac located in the roof of the mouth of dogs and other species of animals, that is not found in man. It was first described by the neuroanatomist Jacobson in the nineteenth century and so is sometimes referred to as the Organ of Jacobson. It is the receptor organ for the "third" chemical sense system that specializes in volatile acids from sexual secretions of the female. For instance, watch a sexually aroused male dog sniff the ground, then begin to salivate and perhaps chomp his jaws. He is engaging in what ethologists call *flehmen*, which is also an activity common to horses, deer and other animals. As the dog chomps, small quantities of saliva are forced by the tongue into the vomeronasal organ, where they come into contact with neuroreceptors. A tooth-chattering display of *flehmen* can be a source of amusement to human onlookers because it seems that the animal is ecstatic. We should envy dogs their vomeronasal sensations!

## Touch

The social conventions that govern where and when people may touch one another do not, as you may have noticed, apply to dogs. Touch receptors are especially concentrated at the base of hair follicles. On other parts of our bodies not covered in hair, like lips, nipples and hands, feet and paws, specialized corpuscles of nerves are congregated which have a selective sensitivity to touch, painful stimuli or extremes of hot and cold. There are wide individual differences between dogs in their touch sensitivity, just as there are systematic differences between breeds. I know of an English bull terrier that was virtually disemboweled by running onto an iron stanchion with sharp projections and yet it seemed not to feel a thing; while I have seen an otherwise macho German shepherd cringe and scream at the mere approach of a hypodermic syringe. There is considerable variation in sensitivity on different parts of the body, though the skin on the inside of the hind leg, around the muzzle, the neck and the pads of the feet is always sensitive to touch. Individual dogs have their own touch zones that give particular pleasure when stimulated, and massage can be usefully formalized into a reward system for training (see page 42).

## SOUND

The world of human communication is primarily a world of sound, which has led us to believe that it is also the natural medium for contact with our dogs. In fact, dogs and their wolf ancestors have only a limited vocal repertoire, and it is probably wrong to assume that much precise information is contained in their growls, grunts, whines, yaps and barks. I believe that we put too much emphasis upon delivering commands by voice. When dogs are trained using visual and postural signals rather than or as well as sound signals, the efficiency of training is greatly enhanced. That is why I discourage excessive use of the voice in dog training, but go instead for the dumb-mute approach, or a combination of voice and gesture.

During domestication and selective breeding, man has given dogs a variety of ear shapes and sizes. Nature intended them to prick up and move: animated antennae to focus upon the source of sound. Both man and dogs are sensitive to a broad spectrum of sounds, varying in frequency from a few cycles per second of infrasound to the ultrasonic 24–25 KHz range. Few humans can hear this upper range, yet most dogs respond to ultrasound. Certain breeds, such as collies, are extraordinarily sensitive to high-frequency sounds, and this can be exploited in training with signals from either a "silent whistle" or an electronic emitter (see page 127).

Most humans overstimulate their pets with sound, delivering commands more loudly than is justified. Always speak softly to your pet and do not imagine that a harsh, guttural voice is more effective than a calm one.

## VISION

Man is first and foremost a visual animal; the dog is to a lesser degree, but most dogs do have good eyesight. Dogs communicate an immense variety of emotions and intents by body posture, lip displays, position and movement of the tail, hair on the nape of the neck (hackles), eye and ear position: they literally have a body language. Since they tend to be shortsighted, their visual world is a more close-contact affair than man's, and they are very efficient at detecting movement, giveaway signs of potential prey or approaching danger. Both people and dogs adapt only moderately to near-darkness, with nighttime vision less well-developed than in truly nocturnal species like cats.

Experiments by the Swedish army in the 1960s showed that it was quite practical, even more efficient, to train dogs for specialized functions using only hand signals and facial gestures, and I have trained a variety of deaf dogs in this way with consistently pleasing results. The exception is the recall signal that is used to obtain a dog's attention when it is looking away, obviously impossible with a deaf dog. In a dog with normal hearing, spoken commands should ideally be used as occasional, supplementary signals to reinforce visual signs.

One attraction of using a primarily visual communication system is that the dog is compelled to watch you, waiting for the next sign from his friend. Owners who complain that their pet is aloof and unresponsive to spoken commands should try placing greater emphasis upon visual signals. When I adopted my Irish setter Sam as a two-year-old, he was definitely the most selectively obedient dog I have ever lived with. He changed to become a model of canine attentiveness when I made a point of ensuring that it was in his own best interests to keep a close eye upon me. A wave to Sam always means something good, so he keeps me within sight—unlike most setters, whose exasperated owners have to bellow into silent woods, ever hopeful of Rover's return!

## DOG TALK

The rapidity of information exchange between a pair of dogs always baffles humans, even people like me who have been studying dogs for years. We naturally focus upon the visual signs: the curl of the lips, tails, ears and so on, missing out on pulses of smell from under the tail, taste from inside the mouth and quiet canine burblings from other orifices. But how can we recognize such signs in a tailless corgi or in an Old English sheepdog that has its eyes covered with hair? With great difficulty! However, most of us develop an amazing ability to recognize our own dog's feelings and likely next move, even without the benefit of a Ph.D. in animal behavior.

The term "metacommunication" has been coined by scientists to plug the hole in our understanding of what dogs are saying to one another: it means that a signal or statement can acquire different meanings according to the context in which it is presented. An intense stare, a growl and scratching of the ground with hind legs acquires an entirely different meaning when delivered after a play bow, compared with the same actions not preceded by a lighthearted bow or low tail wag. Unless we are constantly observant we will miss these rich subtleties of context. If you have access to a video camera, I recommend you film your dog performing such behaviors as playing, threatening, feeding or greeting, and play them back in slow motion. It will show you what metacommunicatory gems you have missed while watching your dog behave in real time.

Whenever you can, put yourself into the dog's coat and position. Get down to ground level, close your eyes and smell the earth. Look up at people who tower over you and ignore their color: dogs live in a world of black, gray and white. Most of all, forget about money, ego and tomorrow; think only of today and of food, warmth, company and sex. In a dog's world it is only today that matters.

# 2

# Individual Differences:
## *The Roots of Eccentricities*

When it comes to educating children, the trend nowadays is to tailor the teaching to the pupil, to encourage confidence and creativity, and to make learning a pleasure. These are the same priorities in my approach to teaching dogs, so different from the old ideas of conformist classrooms or obedience schools for dogs. It sometimes seems to parents that the graduates from modern schools are anarchical and even difficult to govern, but at least they have bold personalities, distinctive tastes and will cope with future change. And so it should be with our dogs. My approach need not be a harbinger of canine chaos because the final limits of what the dog can and can't do still have to be set by a person, but the methods of training are chosen to extend rather than to suppress individual personality.

The pleasure of living with dogs lies less in their appearance than in the things they do and the ways they behave. If selective breeding has created so many standard molds for the appearance of purebreeds, there is still plenty of variety and idiosyncrasy in the ways dogs perform. Ophelia is a Jack Russell terrier who climbs trees as skillfully as a cat; she has a compulsion to be up there in the branches, the higher the better, come rain or shine! She has been "rescued" on many occasions by her caring owners, who once even called the firemen when she scaled a particularly mighty oak, but nothing would deter her. No one trained or encouraged Ophelia to do this; it is just her special quirk that saddled her owners with a combination of worry and pride—liabilities with laughs.

It is striking how tolerant owners are of their pets' foibles. Where do these variations or individual differences come from? They are, of course, part genetic and part learned: both processes leave ample scope for the chance to devise unique, usually winning combinations.

Play is the activity we enjoy most in our dogs, and remarkably they carry on playing from the first weeks of puppyhood to the final days of old age. Most other animals stop playing when they grow up, as I have discovered when trying to jolly up the lives of sows, old polar bears and horses. Even wolves become fairly stuffy creatures at about a year old, yet dogs keep on playing. Why? The answer has been convincingly provided by American biologist Dr. Ray Coppinger, who has established that modern dogs are really perpetual wolf cubs whose behavioral development has been arrested at five months of age. Looking simply at the physical development of the dog, Zeuner coined the term neotony to describe the precocious sexual maturity of domestic dogs compared with their wild ancestors. They are different sides of the same behavioral coin: a dog can be regarded either as a wolf puppy that breeds young or a mature wolf that never grows old!

Some breeds of dogs are definitely more wolflike than others. For instance, the Spitz breeds, which include Samoyeds, malamutes, corgis and Akitas, are closer to the ancestral type in both appearance and behavior, and they tend to be more vocal and more vocally expressive than, say, hounds or terriers. Compare the large vocal repertoire of a wolf or Spitz breed of dog, containing many variations of barks, whines, grumbles and mewls, with the repetitive yapping of many terriers or the monotonous woof of a Pyrenean mountain dog.

Kennel clubs around the world have breed standards, but unfortunately they are written in such general and platitudinous terms that they are often meaningless in relation to behavior. If one believes what one reads, all breeds turn out to be loyal, fun-loving, adaptable and "marvelous with children," with no mention of any negative characteristics. Most breeds available today have changed in appearance, structure and behavior from their working ancestors. And because of inbreeding, the character of a breed can change rapidly: for instance, the Old English sheepdog of the 1950s was very different from today's version. Such changes are especially likely to accompany a marked rise or fall in the popularity of the breed: declining breeds tend to improve, newly trendy breeds to deteriorate. Then there are geographical differences: Dobermans in the U.K. are usually soft, sweet-tempered and comfort-loving, with a definite reluctance to perform complicated, physically demanding activities. By comparison, their "working" cousins in the U.S. and in Germany really can stop unwelcome visitors in their tracks. For this breed as for many others, the type of dog you have depends upon the lines of its ancestors, for example, from German Schutzhund rather than British show stock. But Dobermans everywhere tend to fall asleep on their feet, bang into people, and just a few display a uniquely Doberman compulsion to suck their flanks.

Isolated populations of dogs, such as exist in the United Kingdom, Australia, New Zealand, Iceland and elsewhere, are likely to suffer a more dramatic genetic drift than the same breeds in countries where there is no quarantine or restriction on entry. The prospective puppy-owner should not necessarily assume that the breed of dog they are choosing today is the same as the dogs they knew in childhood. That can be good news for some, bad for others. My particular concern is what is happening to the temperament of golden retrievers in the 1990s. From the reliable family pet of the 1960s and 1970s, they have suddenly taken the top position in referrals to the Animal Behaviour Centre, with sometimes savage aggression. Other breeds have improved their temperament: a mere decade has seen English cockers and German shepherds pose fewer problems of aggression and nervousness than during the 1980s.

Experiments on animals confirm the consensus among medical clinicians that events before birth profoundly influence later development of emotionality and personality. Studies in the 1960s showed that stress in pregnant rats from trauma or overcrowding precipitated development of excessive fear and a tendency to overreact to novel stimuli in their offspring. Similarly, we now know that poor diet and impaired fetal blood supply caused by smoking and other abnormal behavior in mothers can have a deleterious effect upon the physical and intellectual development of human children. In research at the Animal Behaviour Centre, we have shown that puppies bred on "puppy mills" tend to produce offspring that are more emotional and insecure when they grow up than puppies purchased directly from a breeder. Such puppies are mass-produced for profit in crowded and unsanitary conditions, then shipped to distant cities for sale. Their pre-

and postnatal stresses leave a distinct mark upon the puppies' personalities when they eventually become someone's pet.

Another source of individual difference in dogs is the position they occupy along the uterine horn: next to a brother, next to a sister, between two brothers or between two sisters. There is now evidence of a significant sharing or mixing of fetal blood supply in animals like the dog that produce several young in a litter. A female adjacent to males will, to a small extent, be masculinized by her brothers' fetal androgens, while a male that develops between two fetal brothers will be more masculine than one juxtaposed between fetal sisters.

Sex and reproduction are big and interesting topics, and the dog has been one of the favorite species for scientists to study as a model for sexual physiology and behavior in humans. Professor Frank Beach and colleague Dr. Richard Doty, at the University of California, Berkeley, have made some elegant behavioral studies on sex in beagles, one of their findings being that it is female dogs more than male dogs who choose the mate. Long-term friendships between a male and a female usually translated into courtship and mating when they were sexually mature. Contrary to popular belief about canine promiscuity, dogs or at least beagles may favor monogamy if given the chance.

Then there is the belief that it is only the dominant male who mates the female in heat. Wrong again! It is not the dominant male who sets the sexual agenda. Charm rather than power seemed to be the key personality trait of a much-mated beagle, which may explain why mongrels, whose parents choose one another, tend to be such agreeable companions.

Beach and Doty also studied the effects of castration at various ages upon the sexual performance of male dogs at later ages. It seems that male versus female gender roles are primed early and even before birth, but after birth it does not much matter whether a dog is castrated at seven days of age, seven months or seven years. Removal of testosterone (by castration) or replacement therapy with synthetic androgens has the same effects of decreasing or increasing sexual activity at any age of castration.

Finally, there is the question of pleasure: do dogs enjoy sex, do they "need" it? The unhelpful answers to both questions is probably yes and no! Some dogs develop an extraordinary sex drive and will risk everything to be with a female in season, whereas others seem not to be interested in sex at all. Some dogs, usually of miniature breeds like dachshunds and Jack Russells, are sexually active at twelve to sixteen weeks of age; larger breeds, like Great Danes or wolfhounds, may only begin to stir in their second year of life.

People can be very sensitive about such sexual deviancy in their pet. I was recently consulted by a veterinarian whose female cavalier mounted bricks with male-like passions, cocked her leg on lampposts and generally possessed a mixed-up canine gender. These masculine behaviors all appeared after she had been spayed, a surgical procedure which removes what endocrinologists refer to as ovarian suppression of latent male characteristics which had originally been programmed by exposure to fetal androgens. I explained to my veterinarian friend that her puppy's behavior arose from control by as few as twenty-six mislabeled cells in the cerebral cortex. Since they were well out of reach of both drugs and scalpel, I advised that it would be best to put up with her depraved spaniel and look for the funny side.

Then there is the competitive chaos of life within the litter, the fight for access to the most productive nipples, exposure to cold stress, being trodden upon accidentally by the mother, and the host of other things that can go wrong even in the best-run kennels. In the real world, dogs are like children, and they both seem to be remarkably resilient to such early challenges. Coincidentally, these inevitable traumas help to create the individual differences that I can see and appreciate in my otherwise identical twin sons, just as a breeder can see differences in puppies from the same litter. Genetics is always a game of chance, but brothers and sisters have more similar personalities than unrelated animals. It was the Swedish psychologist Anders Hallgren who showed that if you want to know about the likely temperament of a puppy you should examine siblings from previous matings of the same parents.

That may be sound advice in relation to purebred dogs, but it doesn't work for mongrels. Any crossbreeding produces a host of new, random combinations of genes, and members of the same litter of mongrels can all look and behave completely differently from one another. The rule for prospective owners of mongrel puppies is that you may be in for a big surprise.

Another source of individual differences in dogs is the age at which they are taken from breeders. Stimulation during infancy has been demonstrated by scientists to be an important factor which can accelerate physical and mental development. Gentling, by picking up and stroking with the hands, can produce body-weight gains of 10 to 20 percent and accelerate behavioral development by a distinctive margin. A Dutch worker claims that anointing puppies aged between seven and ten days with human underarm sweat improved their subsequent bonding and attachment to people when they were finally placed in homes as pets.

Our corgi Squirrel Nutkins (Nutty to her friends) has a passion for licking feet, mine in particular. As a seven-week-old puppy she had cuddles from all my family, and I don't recollect encouraging her to lie on my old socks! Nutty's breeder is a lady whose husband is a restrained British banker, whom I can't imagine anointing puppies with sweat from armpits, feet or anywhere else. For some, but not for me, it might be a source of professional embarrassment not having all the answers when asked for "expert" advice by the likes of columnist Nigel Dempster, whose Pekingese constantly humps his left foot. I watched and listened to the ecstatic little dog but really can't explain why she does what she does: what goes on in the head of that demented foot-fetishist?

Contemporary thinking in the world of dogs is following a remarkably similar course to that in the world of nursery-school education, where setting a baby on an optimum learning regime creates the best prospects for adult achievement. Puppy playgroups are "in," with all the fun and chaos that the phrase implies, while conformist classes for tough teenage dogs are "out." But what constitutes an optimum early environment? Undoubtedly, a puppy should have contact with a wide variety of human beings of all shapes, colors and ages. Then there are other species—cats, horses, chickens and also other dogs—which it should ideally be exposed to from the age of five to six weeks. An upmarket breeding establishment may not be ideal because it may lack some of these enriching stimuli. Excessive concern with disease control and hygiene might ensure higher survival, but it can be a handicap for good behavioral development. The best compromise is probably the individual breeder with just a few dogs, kept in his or her home, which are bred out of conscientious interest.

I am often asked what is the best age at which to adopt a puppy from a breeder. There is no one answer to this, much depending upon the circumstances in which the puppy is maintained and where its final home will be. For instance, if the breeder is admirably equipped with time, an enriched social environment and an instructive mother dog, it is better that the puppy stays where it is until a later age, say twelve weeks. That is especially true if the adoptive home will be quiet, with the puppy left on his own for long periods and without vital social

stimulation. On the other hand, a breeder offering a relatively institu-
tionalized environment should ensure that puppies are adopted at as
early an age as possible. That is the tried and tested policy of the U.K.
Guide Dogs for the Blind Association, whose puppies go to homes at
the age of six weeks so that they are exposed to all the traumas and
diseases of the real world in preparation for their later role.

Some American dog trainers, leaning on early work by Scott, Fuller,
Fox and others, have argued that it is possible to predict the likely
personality of an adult dog by examining and formally testing it at
seven weeks. The training literature is replete with this and that
regime of "puppy aptitude" testing, but none has been shown to have
any useful predictive qualities, except perhaps by examining grown-
up brothers and sisters from previous matings. Unfortunately, many
dog clubs in America and some European countries still cling to the
hope of making a better match of a puppy to its prospective owner.
However, research by myself and by Dr. Margaret Young of Duke
University, North Carolina, has shown that there is no scientific basis
to puppy testing, which means that sadly many puppies have been
rejected as unsuitable for pet-keeping at too early an age, without
being given a chance to develop.

Puppies may have no choice in the genetic code on their chromo-
somes, but they soon make an impact upon that other fate-maker,
people. I am often told anecdotes by owners who believe that their
puppy or rescued dog "chose" them, that they felt irrevocably drawn,
there was love at first sight and so on. Be that as it may, owners assume
the privileged role of guardian to their puppy, and it is remarkable
how the young canine personality is modified from then on.

Julian and Spot were border collie brothers who were brought to
me by their separate families because the dogs constantly barked at
one another through the fence between their adjoining properties.
If they met away from home the dogs were friendly toward one another. Aside from the challenge of sorting out an interesting case of
friction between neighbors, I was struck by the contrast of personality
between the two dogs. Spot was nervous, given to submissive roll-over
displays when greeting strangers, and he even urinated involuntarily
when greeted by his own family. Julian was hale and hearty with all
comers; bouncy and chaotic, he was liable to ruin the best clothes of
any humans in his life. Yet on their own, and with my assistant Sam,
the two dogs were indistinguishable. Their differences lay, I believe,
almost entirely in the attributes of the respective owners.

Spot had ended up with a conformist, discipline-orientated and rather dull owner who fancied his hand at "working" competitive sheep dog trials. He believed that a dog should "know his place, should not be spoiled and be given a purpose in life." Julian's family were just ordinary, liberal folk who treated him as one of the family and asked only that he sit at curbs and come when called. Spot lived in a world of constant "no" and "leave," whereas Julian was surrounded by people whom he could manipulate and who knew how to give and receive love.

Occasionally, the very smallest thing can ruin some aspect of a puppy's future. The first car journey from breeder to new home for a puppy often provokes motion sickness or vomiting, which may then set the scene for a long-term psychological problem about car travel. An encounter between a new puppy and a crotchety old cat can leave a lifetime's impression upon the dog, fueling either fear or fury toward all the world's felines.

An unexpected setback like running into a glass door as a puppy attempts to follow his owner on the other side can temporarily disrupt his bond and interest in people as effectively as a cruel smack on the nose. My eight-week-old setter puppy Pollo gave us a perfect illustration of such one-trial learning when he was startled by the metallic thud of the spring catch on a gate in a field near our house. Months later Pollo still won't walk through the open gate, though he will crawl under when it is closed.

The presence of another dog in the house is likely to be the major learning influence upon a young puppy. I witness this every day as little Pollo attempts to copy ten-year-old Sam. Suave Sam is a role model for the puppy, to the extent of "teaching" him to lift his right but not his left paw in play, to howl on a cue from humans, to respect horses' hooves and not to chase chickens. Mimicry or associative learning is a powerful factor in puppy development and an only dog is at an obvious disadvantage to a puppy that is surrounded by others. That is why I urge my clients to introduce their puppy to suitable canine role models at as early an age as possible: if you have to, borrow the best adult dogs you know from neighbors, friends or family.

Every day I see dogs for whom everything seemed to have begun right, yet who present unexpected problems of nervousness, aggression or disobedience. Many dogs also come my way who have an unhappy history yet behave well. So don't panic if you are unable to achieve perfect conditions for your pet: most dogs cope very well with adversity. Equally important is not to soul search and breast beat if your dog develops some irritating habit or dangerous trait. Rather than blame yourself, read on to find my positive solutions, or seek professional help.

The purpose of this book is to let every dog develop his potential within the lives of the people around him. The message to you, the reader, is not to force conformity upon your dog, but rather to encourage him to develop into a unique, fantastic canine character. To be a very special dog!

# 3
# Animal Learning:
## *A Sponge for Knowledge*

Owing to a careless mistake by his owner, my first Irish setter once caught his tail in a revolving door, which though undoubtedly painful caused him no physical injury. Bip was two years old at the time, and for the remaining fifteen years of his life he would always pause and await confirmation from a human that a door was safe to pass through. A single adverse experience had produced a permanent change in Bip's behavior.

In my professional work helping owners to stop their pets engaging in undesirable habits, I am constantly amazed at the speed with which dogs learn new associations, habits or tricks. If they were not so easily trained, one supposes that they would not have been domesticated in the first place, nor would they have achieved their present-day popularity. And yet many owners seem to experience difficulty in teaching their dogs, writing them off as untrainable. Many more attend training classes for weeks, months and even years, repeating boring rote exercises to ever more precise standards. The truth is that dog training need not require sustained effort from trainers or be boring to the dog: there is an easier way! Before describing this, we need to understand how animals learn.

Psychologists distinguish between short-term and long-term

memory: there seem to be distinctive physiological mechanisms for the two phenomena, so that events stored in short-term memory are easily "wiped," confused or forgotten, but are securely stored when entered into long-term memory. Short-term memory is thought by scientists to be the product of complex reverberating electrical circuits in the cortex of the brain, that at some point enter into the second learning stage of long-term memory. It is thought that the transfer of information from short-term to long-term memory occurs during REM, or dream sleep, when potent images are experienced by humans and probably also by dogs. This second stage of memory has a chemical basis, involving coding onto proteins which can be read in a manner analogous to digital sequences on a compact disc.

Once committed to long-term store, only profound and damaging events can erase this chemical transcription of memory or interfere with its recall. For instance, long-term memory can resist electric shock therapy, traumatic injury to the brain, even repeated epileptic fits, but is lost in medical conditions such as Alzheimer's disease where the nerve cells have irrevocably deteriorated.

Returning to Bip, my setter, in the last half-year of his life and until he died at seventeen and a half, there were many signs of such degenerative changes in his behavior, but one of them was positive: he forgot his lifetime fear of doors. The transcriptor mechanism of long-term memory had worked too well for Bip in his prime, but old age finally liberated him.

There have been many theories of learning by authors from Aristotle onward, but let us start with the pioneering German, Hermann Ebbinghaus, who believed that learning occurs by a process of linkage or association between events, syllables and numbers. At about the same time, in the late nineteenth century, the famous trainer and writer Konrad Most, a compatriot of Ebbinghaus, applied the same theoretical notions of learning by association to dogs. Colonel Most devised the concept of training by inducements, which might be positive if they were rewarding; more commonly they were negative or punishing and involved application of force. Unfortunately, while psychology has moved on to more sophisticated models of learning in both man and animals, dog training has tended to remain rooted in the rather elementary and military approach handed down from Colonel Most.

The next "great leap forward" in our understanding of the process and structural basis of memory came from Russian neurophysiologists, particularly Ivan Pavlov, who worked in St. Petersburg. Two experiments in particular have entered the popular folklore about animal learning: salivation by dogs conditioned to the sound of a pre-meal bell, and sheep showing a conditioned leg movement in response to a signal which preceded the administration of electric shock. Pavlov provided us with useful terminology to describe what went on with the behavior of his dogs, sheep and other experimental subjects. The "unconditioned response" is the natural reaction of the body to a particular stimulus, an "unconditioned stimulus." For example, the unconditioned response of a hungry dog to the unconditioned stimulus of food is to salivate: the unconditioned response of a sheep to the unconditioned stimulus of electric shock is to struggle and endeavor to escape. These unconditioned responses are somatic or bodily reactions, in one case of the mouth and alimentary tract, in the other of the peripheral muscles regulating movement. After several sessions in which the dog or sheep was given prior exposure to the conditioned stimulus of bell or buzzer, it began to evoke qualitatively similar responses of salivation (in the dog) and leg lift (in the sheep) as had previously been evoked by food or electric shock. A new conditioned response had been formed by a process that psychologists have termed classical conditioning. The Pavlovian learning system is summarized in the diagram on the next page.

The classical condition paradigm is especially useful in understanding the development of extreme fearful responses to otherwise neutral stimuli, for instance to unusual sounds such as the hiss of brakes on trucks, or an overreaction to the sounds of distant gunshot. In dog training by traditional methods which use the choke chain, classical conditioning is also the principal mechanism for learning, where commands such as "heel," "down" or "leave" are conditioned stimuli to the unconditioned stimulus of pain from a harshly yanked choke chain. This may seem to be a practical approach in training classes, but it is largely irrelevant to the real world of dogs performing complex and natural behavior.

If only relatively simple actions or habits are learned by classical conditioning, how are more complex behaviors such as herding sheep or opening a refrigerator to steal food learned? Some of the answers are to be found in the rather specialized and jargon-ridden literature of instrumental learning, where rats run mazes and press levers, pigeons peck lights or monkeys press buttons. I spent three years studying this rather dry literature as a psychology undergraduate, and

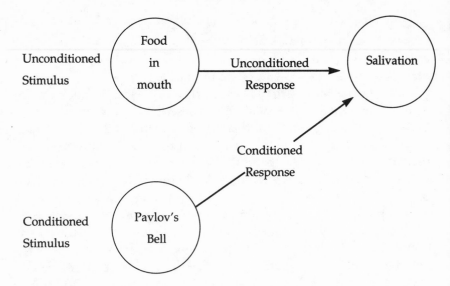

*Figure 1. Classical or Pavlovian conditioning of a dog to the sound of a bell before food.*

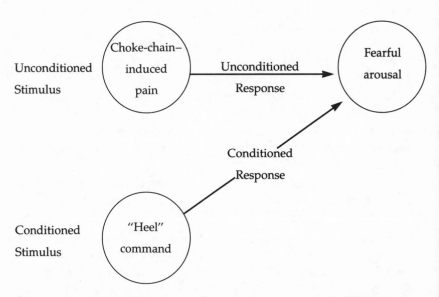

*Figure 2. Classical conditioning to train a dog not to pull on the leash. Pain from the choker and the "Heel" command become equivalent stimuli, with similar physiological responses of fear.*

despite unpromising first appearances, there really are some useful scientific principles of learning ripe for application to dog training. But I needed the inspiration of a Devon shepherd to make the necessary theoretical connections.

Jim Burgoyne took sheep and cattle across, in and out of the county; he was probably the last of Devon's drovers. He worked alone, except he had the help of a motley crew of dogs: five to ten collies with this and that mixed in, who shared what must have been one of the best lives on earth. The cattle trucks took all Jim's long-distance work, but he remained indispensable on Dartmoor where only his dogs could collect and move large flocks of flighty Dartmoor and Scottish blackface sheep. People in his hometown of Ivybridge kept bequeathing Jim their worst-behaved problem pets because all could see that his dogs idolized him. What was the secret?

I spent a happy half-day in 1981 with Jim Burgoyne and his dogs on the moors, just listening and looking. Rule 1 was to stay quiet so as not to distract the dogs. Rule 2 seemed to be "let the dogs get on with it, be their own teachers." Jim pointed out the copycat behaviors of young or new dogs following old and established pack members. Learning the droving ropes took only a few days for a new dog, but it was the other dogs more than Jim who were the teachers. Rule 3 seemed to be kindness: keep all the dogs on Jim's side so they wouldn't be tempted to run off and into trouble. Finally, Rule 4 was to carry a pocketful of disgusting-smelling dried meat for reward, and a catapult to interrupt any unacceptable deviation such as chicken killing or cat chasing. If the dog did it right, Jim was there with his meat; if he did it wrong, a pebble hit the ground with a whack! No shouting or reprimands and little verbal praise, just the dogs' names called to maintain cohesion within the pack: "contact calls" in the vocabulary of ethology.

I realized that Jim Burgoyne's training system was as sophisticated as anything attempted before by psychologists with complex animals like Washoe, the chimp who was taught to communicate with people in American Sign Language. Instrumental learning was more than just rat-running in a psychology laboratory. Back to theory!

We have to thank cats and the American researcher Edward Thorndike for the earliest insights into how dogs and other animals might learn complex tasks. He confined cats to a cage fitted with a lock that could, with difficulty, be opened by the animal, so that it could obtain food or join other cats. He called this his "puzzle box" and noticed that cats acquired the correct sequence of escape moves in a gradual fashion by a process of trial and error. To make a successful escape, the cat had to experiment or to fiddle with the latch: no one and nothing guided it, and it was always free to give up or continue its efforts at escape. Simply put, the cat rather than Professor Thorndike was in control. But like Jim Burgoyne's dogs, Thorndike noticed that his cats would copy one another if given the chance.

So could instrumental techniques work on the dog? The strange thing is that although a comprehensive and minutely detailed series of experiments have explored instrumental learning by other animals and man, psychologists have simply neglected to offer the fruits of their labors to the poor old dog. He has been stuck with chokers attached to trainers flexing overgrown biceps doing it the Most way, while cats and children have been allowed to learn by discovery. My aim in life is to give all dogs the lucky break that Jim Burgoyne had given to his Devonshire dogs.

The first requirement for instrumental learning is patience and a sharp eye, because the dog controls the time, place and speed of the learning process. Let's illustrate the approach by example. You own a five-door hatchback and you want to train your dog to jump in by the rear door, not by the four side doors. Sit in the front of the car, having first placed a bowl of food in the rear luggage compartment and shut all doors except the rear one. Your dog will approach, either out of greed or the prospect of your company. As his front paws are placed in the car, say "Up," and when he spontaneously jumps in, say "In," and reward him by allowing him to eat the food. Repeat the procedure two or three times, then stand beside the car and offer the same "up" and "in" commands from a distance, as your dog spontaneously performs the desired action. Pretty soon your dog will jump into your car only after you give the "up-in" commands. You will have achieved instrumental control by labeling the desired behavior of getting into the car with some simple commands. Look at the example in Figure 3.

Instrumental learning need not just involve the use of rewards; unpleasant associations can follow actions which the trainer might not wish the dog to perform. Taking the car example, once the dog has learned to enter via the rear door through positive reinforcement, you may now want his options for entry narrowed to that door alone, completely excluding the option of the side doors. Maybe you have a remote-controlled car alarm installed, or rig up some tin cans to rattle inside the car as your dog makes his first cautious but "wrong" entry

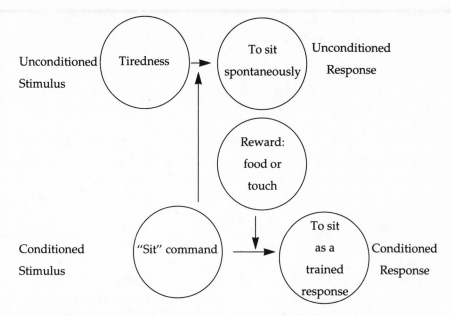

*Figure 3. Instrumental training of "sit." The dog naturally sits when it is tired. By "labeling" that unconditioned response with the conditioned stimulus "Sit!" and then rewarding it, we induce a conditioned response of sitting. The dog is always in control: he is "instrumental" in the outcome.*

through the side door. Alternatively, it may have been sufficient "punishment" that he did not get to the food in the back except by the rear door. But care is needed in the use of punishment, even in the simple example given. You, the "punisher," need to be hidden and silent, or your dog will be frightened of you or only avoid the side doors when you are around. Secondly, do not make the punishment so extreme that it produces a general aversion to the car. Finally, be sure that the timing of punishment perfectly coincides with the act of entry into the car, not with sitting inside on the seats.

To summarize, here are the key features of instrumental learning that were illustrated by the car example:

• The trainer stayed quiet and seemingly independent of any negative aspects.
• The word "no" was not used as a secondary reinforcer: it is so often the all-purpose "devil" for dogs during training and would be better dropped from the vocabulary.

- Timing is everything, be it for reward or punishment: more than a few seconds late and the wrong instrumental act may be "credited" or "debited."
- The action which is being trained by instrumental methods has to come naturally to the dog and it must not be inherently unpleasant to him.

This is a good restraint upon over-the-top trainers who might be tempted to make an animal do something bizarre or dangerous, such as an elephant sitting on a barrel lifting a live tiger; or a dog jumping through a burning hoop, so often a part of displays with German shepherds.

It is not just simple behaviors that can be trained using instrumental techniques. Even guide dogs can be trained using these methods, according to a recent book by the blind British psychologist Bruce Johnson. It seems that so far as complexity is concerned, the sky is the limit! The technical term "shaping" needs to be borne in mind, meaning that an animal's behavior can be shaped in a series of small or simple steps toward a complex ultimate goal; for example, wanting to train a dog to wipe his own paws on a particular towel reserved for that purpose, to save you a chore at the end of a walk. I might add that I have not yet succeeded in training Sam to do this, but it is only through lack of commitment on my part! This is a fun project that will take a little time, and we must decide in advance that it can only be achieved by positive reinforcement; punishment will just make the dog opt out of wiping his paws. Let's try the following strategy.

Most dogs at some stage scrape the ground in chemical marking. Give the activity a label such as "scrape" and bring it under instrumental control by consistent reinforcement. When there is a 100 percent reliability of obtaining the scrape response to the command "scrape," lay out a towel on the ground near where the dog customarily performs this behavior. Transfer the scrape behavior onto the towel, then gradually relocate the towel bit by bit closer to the door of your house. Having obtained the dog's willingness to scrape on the towel by the door, you might care to go one step further and have him take down the towel from a hook. This next phase is called "chaining," when we link together the first habit of scraping with the second habit of taking a towel off the wall.

Chaining is the means by which a dog can be trained to perform seemingly remarkable and complex tasks, such as guiding a blind person from home to office across dangerous streets, locating drugs in suitcases on an airport conveyor belt or opening a door for the physically disabled. To help understand how the dog can be trained to perform such useful jobs we need to take on board the psychological term "shaping." Shaping is essentially the concept of a little at a time, making big tasks easy by breaking them into small components which are then linked or "chained" in a practical and convenient sequence.

Finally, I will delve into one more element of the jargon about learning in animals, the notion of "schedules of reinforcement." This term refers to the frequency and the predictability of rewarding or punishing the animal for his performance. If every time a dog lifts his paw he receives a tidbit, this is known as "continuous reinforcement." However, the trainer may decide only to reward every second or every fifth paw lift: an "intermittent schedule of reinforcement." In this last example, animal psychologists can specify the manner of reward more precisely by the notation FR 2 or FR 5: a "fixed ratio" of reward on every second or fifth response respectively.

Intermittent reinforcement can be made yet more unpredictable by introducing a variable time element: a so-called "variable interval" schedule where, for instance, only a paw lift at one-minute intervals will be chosen for reward: a VI 60 ratio. These schedules of reinforcement are of more than academic interest; they have a practical impact upon how quickly something is learned and especially how long before it is forgotten. Many of the everyday behaviors we train in dogs are intermittently reinforced and persist for a long time even without further reward. For instance, the habit of begging for food at the table is easily stimulated by a crumb accidentally dropped from the lap of a diner, but once the begging habit has been rewarded by a combination of FR and VI schedules of reinforcement it will carry on despite little further prospect of more crumbs.

I know the truth of this from living with Sam. Someone, but not a Mugford, years ago fed him a scrap at the table. Sam does not try it with me or our family because we never have nor will relent. But most dinner guests are given the slobbery begging treatment because the habit was started by a visitor, and subsequent visitors have reaped the penalty. In summary, if we consistently reward a dog in the early stages of training, the number and predictability of rewards can be dramatically reduced later on. A dog will then perform like a gambler at his payola machine, ever in hope that the next move will be his lucky one!

4

# Reward vs. Punishment:
## *Tyranny or Tenderness*

Like you and me, dogs are pleasure-seeking individuals, hedonists who if at all possible will avoid hunger, pain, cold, repetitive tedium or threatening company. If the poor dog lives the role of subordinate slave to a dominant master, the use of physical punishment during dog training might seem sensible: for instance, to shake it by the scruff of the neck or to inflict pain from a choke chain. As the reader will now know, I believe that that view of dogs' social organization is fundamentally flawed and owners should almost never openly punish their companion. Instead, we should be loyal friends who protect them from unpleasantness wherever possible. My approach leads to a more interesting relationship between people and their pets and it need not produce chaos.

## REWARDS

Dogs still have to be trained to "fit in" with humans, so what are the factors which turn them on: which are the key rewards for a dog, or as a psychologist would say, the best positive reinforcers?

## Warmth

The newborn puppy's journey from its mother's birth canal to the nipple is principally based upon a search for warmth, and indeed very young puppies consistently move from cool to warm spots in order to increase their body temperature. A newborn puppy is unable to regulate its body temperature as efficiently as an adult dog, so it relies upon external sources to maintain the target 102° F.

An adult wolf can readily withstand extreme low temperatures, which in Arctic areas can go down to minus 40° F. By the domestic fireside, piles of dogs will jockey to be roasted by the flames, a particularly common occurrence in the Mugford household. Our dogs' coats have literally scorched in front of an open fire, and when they rise from their slumbers they experience obvious discomfort as the hot hairs touch more sensitive underlying skin. We sometimes speculate as to whether my setter Sam's brains have been scrambled by the repetitive application of local heat, but we need not worry as the brain is well protected from overheating by ample blood circulation.

The quest for warmth explains a great many behavioral quirks. For instance, dogs sit on our laps not only because of their attachment to us, or even from a desire to gain height and dominate us, but for the pleasure of our warm abdomens. A dog's selection of this or that surface in different parts of the house is also determined by small variations in heat conductivity of the floor, deep-pile woolen tufted usually being favored over close-pile synthetics. Of course, there are individual differences: a Pyrenean mountain dog or hairy Newfoundland will usually spurn domestic pleasures, preferring to lie on cold concrete rather than carpet.

## Food

The second important resource for a newborn puppy is its mother's sweet milk. In fact, the responsiveness to sweet stimuli exists in all mammals, even before they are born. Dogs (but not cats) are like people and retain a passion for sugars throughout life. There are other attributes of food besides sweetness that dogs like and need. At the time of weaning, puppies require more complex proteins and other nutrients than are contained in milk, so they develop a marked preference for meat, especially when it is cooked. A preference for cooked cuisine can hardly have a logical evolutionary basis, unless it was smells from man's cookpot which first tempted wolves in from the wild.

The giving of food as tidbits during dog training is sometimes frowned upon, but not in the Mugford way. What matters is the time and manner of its giving, which should occur not because the dog has begged for it, but because it has performed a desirable act at the appropriate time and to the appropriate signal. The quantity of food given can be tiny: the sniff of a crumb is all that is needed for my gluttonous corgi to run a hard race or perform an amazing feat. By way of contrast, my finicky setter Sam demands that any food reward be quite spectacularly tasty if he is to speed up his performance. For Sam, the prospect of play, touch, voice and attention is always more important than food.

About seven out of ten dogs are highly food orientated, enough for it to be practical to train them with tidbits. However, I discourage the use of sugar-based rewards because of their disastrous effects upon oral health and obesity. It is always better to employ a savory snack, of which there are many to choose from: dry cat food pellets are usually more palatable than dog biscuits and both provide balanced nutrition. This approach is especially convenient in dog training because you can calculate the daily ration for your dog by reference to his weight and lifestyle, setting aside a proportion of the daily allowance for use as tidbits during training. In certain complex behavior modification regimes, 60 to 70 percent of the dog's food can come from tidbits; in other dogs, on other tasks, no tidbits at all may be more appropriate.

### Touch

When describing the sense of touch (see page 18) I pointed to the great variations in touch sensitivity on different parts of a dog's body and in different breeds. If you are a warm, tactile person, you will soon discover the body areas that your puppy or dog enjoys having stroked, tickled and massaged. Too many of us give our dogs a perfunctory pat and brief stroke to the head when a harder kneading action may be more appreciated. The base of the ears, chest and hindquarters are usually pleasurable touch zones for the dog, which you should manipulate with the fingers rather than the soft palm of your hand.

Touch and massage create a closer and more affectionate bond between man and dog, so that restraining your dog, say to remove a thorn or to tend to some other injury, will be more likely to be

tolerated. We recently saw an excellent example of the bonding consequences of persistent massage from a guest in our household, an
Icelandic girl who was then deprived of the company of dogs at home,
and overcompensated with my setter Sam. In just two weeks Marta
Guölaugsdóttir converted Sam from being Roger Mugford's best mate
into the adoring disciple of a Nordic blonde!

## Play

Play is an extraordinary behavior and certainly not without purpose.
Scientific study has shown that it is an important mechanism whereby
the young of most species perfect skills in dangerous and complex
activities which may be essential for survival later on. For the wolf and
its dog derivatives, hunting is clearly that dangerous and complex
activity, but play also offers the means for developing social skillfulness.

Each week, I run a puppy playgroup at the Animal Behaviour
Centre, where we see fantastic antics among juvenile dogs as they
unleash immense energy in tag, chase, assault and ear-pulling, followed by gentle sniffing, licking and demonstrations of camaraderie.
Within an hour, distinctive gangs or subgroups have developed within
the class of about fifteen, puppies of like size and temperament usually
coming together. We rarely see coalitions between Jack Russells and
golden retrievers; opposites seem to repel rather than attract. Not all
dogs have this opportunity for gregarious subject play in playgroups:
object play with toys and with people are poor substitutes for dogs
that have to stay at home.

Considerable research has gone into developing appropriate and
safe toys for dogs, though one might not think so when looking at the
dangerous objects sold by some pet stores. The toys that work best are
those which mimic some element of hunting in the wild, like an animal
being chased, and produce a soft mouth-feel when grabbed and given
the "death bite"; they might even taste of meat. Additionally, a
"squeak" noise might simulate the sound of a prey in agony. No one
toy on the market fully combines all these elements, but latex squeaky
toys come near to it by being soft and bouncy, and the noise they make
fascinates dogs. Unfortunately, the cheaper plastic squeaky toys do
not have sufficient resilience to withstand bites and so can be dangerous if the pieces are swallowed. Check your pet's toys constantly
and remove any that show signs of wear and tear. The toy which most

nearly fits the description of an ideal dog toy is the Kong (see page 132), because it stimulates play even without the participation of humans. The Kong is a tough and practical reward to offer as an exciting agitation toy after a dog has successfully performed some complex activity like scentwork.

## Company

Being a social animal, no single resource is more important to the dog than company. You might even be more important to your dog than his food! The smallest increase in interest, availability or time in contact with a dog can be a potent reward; in turn they seek your attention. A stare, a smile or touch that you give spontaneously may have a wealth of subtle meaning to your dog. The corollary to your company being rewarding is that denial of it can be a severe punishment.

## PUNISHMENTS

Animals do not behave as they do simply in order to obtain rewards; they also try to avoid certain situations or outcomes. Psychologists refer to the latter as "negative reinforcers," while the rest of humanity calls them punishments. In fact, punishment is not such a good term, since it has moral connotations associated with criminality and wrongdoing. In dog training, it is best to set aside such thoughts and just focus upon what is practical, what is ethical and what works. A long list of exotic negative reinforcers could be devised, but I will group them under the following headings.

## Pain

Farmers, gamekeepers and others with a robust attitude toward dog training have long used the boot or a twitch to direct dogs away from unwanted activity, but they pay a severe price by losing the dog's respect and affection. In particular, the flinch to a raised hand or boot tells all, and like my Bip's tail trapped by a revolving door, it can take a lifetime for a dog to forget an unpleasant experience.

The most widespread abuse of dogs in training is not from the stick, hand or boot but from the ubiquitous choke chain. The reader will know my feelings on this point already, but suffice it to say here that it disrupts attention and blocks learning. In other words, it is a handicap rather than a help for the dog trainer. Worst of all, the dog relates being jerked on a choker to the trainer and not to the preceding instrumental behavior, so that training with a choke chain carries the high risk of inadvertently alienating the dog from his handler. I saw this in the dramatic case of a rottweiler brought to our Paris clinic in 1985. Bürst had been too strong for his mademoiselle, so she resorted to a pinch collar. Every time he was jerked or punished by pain from the spikes, he mounted his mistress in a way that she believed was sexy, and a trainer believed was dominant-aggressive, but which I interpreted to be a combination of ingratiating appeasement and pain avoidance. Incidentally, the problem ceased the moment Bürst was fitted with a headcollar and the pinch collar discarded.

## Sound

The dog is sensitive to a remarkably wide spectrum of sounds, and certain wavelengths and intensities can provoke distress. High-frequency sound in particular usually upsets herding breeds such as border collies. Occasionally, low-frequency sounds can be upsetting to some dogs. It has been demonstrated by French workers studying the response of beagles to moderately loud, commonplace household sounds that their normal gastrointestinal rhythm was completely disrupted by listening to heavy metal rock music, played at only 86 decibels (dB). This was not loud music by the standards of most teenagers, yet it bothered the dogs. There was a transient rise in cortisol levels, indicating that these dogs really were stressed by the music, even though they showed no outward behavioral signs of suffering.

For behavioral therapy, we often use a variety of unexpected sound stimuli in dog training. My favorite sound-making device is the rattle of a tin can, which combines the perfect attributes of being cheap and easily available—also, we do the world a favor by picking them up!

Another convenient source of negative reinforcement is ultrasound, produced by any number of electronic gadgets in addition to the traditional silent whistle. Unfortunately, the sound output of these devices is generally rather low (40 to 50 dB), so their discouraging effects tend only to be at short range and then mostly in small-headed breeds of dogs. Larger breeds with heavier ethmoid bones require more sound energy to stimulate their sense of hearing and are less reactive to ultrasound. However, I recently saw a Yorkshire terrier that had for years attacked its mistress as she walked across the room to answer the telephone. I found that an ultrasonic alarm consistently interrupted this behavior, saving my client's ankles and providing an opportunity to redirect the said Yorkie into an alternative activity: sitting on a sofa near to but just out of reach of the telephone.

## Social withdrawal

Just as human company is a powerful enticement to most dogs, its withdrawal can be a nasty punishment. Psychologists have long referred to this as "time out," a procedure that many parents will know about in relation to child control. Time out is an especially appropriate form of punishment for aggression or other such complex social behavior. To challenge or take on a threatening powerful dog is usually unwise; better to penalize him by stomping from the room. However, time out is less suitable strategy to discourage minor, frequently repeated behaviors such as barking or jumping up.

A mistake made by many dog-owners (and possibly also by parents) is the assumption that if one minute's separation does the trick, two minutes', twenty minutes' or two hours' should be proportionately even better. The duration of time out should be kept brief, so as to allow the learning experience of cause and effect to be repeated more often. Time out is best used in dog training by walking away from the dog rather than by physically expelling it from the room, because contact with the dog might inadvertently reinforce another undesired activity. The practical aspects of this process may not always be straightforward: if the family want to remain in the den and watch a favorite television program, it can be more punishing for them than for the dog to have to walk out and leave Fido with the TV.

Social withdrawal can be a more subtle and practical means of exerting control than time out; for many dogs, to be ignored is devastating. Simply break eye contact, lift up hands and turn away. In the same category are the punishing signals that particular facial expressions can suggest to a dog. You can probably best convey your disapproval by a calm, steely stare, just as dogs themselves sometimes give the threatening, intimidatory eye.

Equally, tone of voice, particularly a strained-intensity scream, can be deeply upsetting to many sensitive dogs. However, that same scream may excite other dogs to unwanted activity, so choose the strategy which works for you. For many dogs, it is better just to go limp, to stay silent and look away when you want to punish them.

## Water

A spray of water has long been a favorite method to interrupt irritating but minor misdemeanors such as yapping. Of course, for water-loving Labradors a spray may have the opposite effect! As with any form of punishment, surprise is the key to its effectiveness, as was nicely demonstrated to me some years ago by my first red setter, Bip.

We were walking alongside the River Dart on the moors, in the company of a boisterous adolescent male border collie. Bip had been altogether overbearing and threatening to his companion, and was on the point of launching an attack when he missed his footing and fell into the wintry river. He came out strangely humbled toward the little collie and never again initiated an attack upon any dog. The perfection of the occasion was that I was not involved in the delivery of punishment; it was brought on by Bip's own actions and it was well timed.

## Electrical shock

The technology for the controlled delivery of electrical shock to dogs has existed for many years and regrettably is now used to interrupt such commonplace behaviors as barking or straying off the property. They consist of a battery which energizes a high-voltage coil connected to electrodes lying against the dog's neck. A radio-control circuit using CB wavelengths is usually incorporated into the device, with the receiver built into the dog's collar and the transmitter unit held by the trainer. Some shock collars are used to punish barking by being linked to a microphone built into the collar, and others are activated by an induced magnetic field from wire buried around the edge of the property that "zaps" the poor dog if he crosses it. Many designs of shock collar are electrically unsafe, liable to cause burns and severe pain due to malfunction. Others are unreliable and stop working just at the critical moment. It is essential that these devices be fitted with an adjustment to tailor shock intensity to the sensitivity of

the particular dog, or excessive pain will induce long-term patholog-
ical fears.

Regrettably, some hunters train their dogs to retrieve dead birds in a
straight line by setting painful electrical "minefields" if the dog should
deviate from a straight return to the trainer. Generally, the shocking
punishment is delivered without the dog being aware of the trainer's
role in this unseemly torture, though I expect and hope that many
clever dogs break the code and learn to blame people. I am told that
gundogs trained by this method have a tendency either to run away
from shoots, or return in straight lines without the bird!

The practical disadvantage of training with shock collars is that the
unlucky dog is forever searching for a rational basis to the punishment: is it being hurt by a long blade of grass, a passing dog, a strange
human being, a low-flying aircraft? Any of these might be blamed for
the shocks. My conclusion is that the penalty for training with electrical shock collars is the definite possibility of producing a neurotic,
profoundly disturbed dog, and that such devices should have no place
in the homes of caring pet-owners. I will admit to a small specialized
role for shock collars in the modification of predatory behavior, such
as chasing other animals where it can be remarkably effective and life
saving in professional hands. However, as we shall see later, even for
sheep chasing there are simple, low-tech alternative training methods
available, and prevention is always better than cure.

## Odors

We can guess at the power of certain smells as punishment to a dog by
observing their distaste for car exhaust fumes or the taint of furniture
polish. A French invention, the Aboistop (bark-stop), which emits an
odor at the precise moment a dog barks, has opened my eyes to the
potential of olfactory stimulation for discouraging unwanted activity.
One could also deliver odors by a hand-operated aerosol, but the
timing and association would be imperfect and "blamed" upon the
trainer. If you want to try a hand-operated odor-delivery system, bear
in mind that every dog has different likes and dislikes so use trial and
error to find the perfume which is nice to you but discouraging to your
pet! The latest technology of all is a remote-control odor-delivery
system, which can reward or punish with nice or nasty smells at a
distance. Maybe we can harness this device to "talk" in a language

that dogs can understand: blended aromas for every occasion, every emotion!

Finally, there is always the ethical and practical dilemma about whether to punish or to put up with a dog's misdemeanors. I am a bit of a softy in such matters, but based on both theory and practice I am certain that if there is such a dilemma about punishment, don't! After all, a wolf's teeth were designed for killing prey more than for terrorizing partners in the pack. Their lives are regulated by love and loyalty and so should ours be.

# 5

# Training Theory:

## *Instrumental Learning and the Mugford Way*

I take the anarchical view that basic dog training should be no more than a five-minute job for the skilled professional; five hours for the owner of an unruly adult dog and maybe five weeks for the owner of a young puppy. How is such fast work possible, you might ask.

There are certain theoretical principles that will help the reader to achieve these ambitious targets. The approach to teaching known as instrumental learning has been tried and tested on thousands of our canine patients at the Animal Behaviour Centre, and believe me, it is as good for dogs as it is for people!

In Chapter 3, I made the distinction between classical conditioning and operant or instrumental learning. These are the key practical elements of training by instrumental techniques:

*Don't take good behavior for granted.* Most of us have more to do with a dog when it is behaving badly, correcting it by whatever means, settling back and ignoring it when it performs well. Just as with children, what we ought to be offering instead is encouragement. If your dog greets you without jumping up, without barking, or without biting the friendly visitor at the door, acknowledge his good judgment and make a big fuss over him.

*Reward positive behavior immediately.* Any delay between performance of a behavior and its reward greatly weakens the power of the reinforcer—you may inadvertently reward a quite different activity instead. Always carry tidbits and be free with your voice and hands to reinforce behavior at the moment it is performed.

*Reduce reinforcement of long-established habits.* This would seem to be a contradiction of the earlier rule, but it is really quite straight-forward: there is no need consistently to reward every successful performance of an act when we can move to an intermittent reinforcement schedule (see Chapter 3). If food was a primary reinforcer during early training of your dog, you can later gradually wean him off, reducing either the number or the predictability of rewards. At this well-established and skillful stage, his behavior will not be forgotten and the animal will seemingly continue to perform just out of habit.

*Train by small steps.* The most complex task can be broken down into small, self-contained elements that are easily learned. That is how dogs have been trained to guide the blind, alert the deaf, find bodies and even ride skateboards.

When training a chain or sequence of such activities, try to train the last step first. This must sound like double-dutch when common sense tells us that it is best to teach the first elements of a task first. Not so. If you have reinforced earlier stages of the chain, the dog might want to stop and await his payoff before reaching the final stage. For instance, if the task is to run away and collect objects strewn over a hillside, the first element to be trained is to drop objects, closely followed by the recall, or "come." The next step in the chain will be to teach the dog to pick up objects, to move to left or right by hand signals, to run away from the handler and so on.

*Shaping: build on good behavior.* Shaping involves gradually changing the definition of what constitutes desired behavior: for instance, greater speed, longer duration of performance or distance from the handler at which a task is performed. Usually, the trainer builds upon an existing habit rather than starting from scratch. For instance, training a dog to operate a seesaw could begin with the habit of a dog already trained to run along a horizontal plank, and only at the end need it be trained to balance around the central fulcrum. This technique of training animals is usually described as "shaping," but psychologists dealing with skills training in people also call it the method of "successive approximation."

*Better to substitute than to punish.* I have already referred to the disruptive consequences of punishment, even when given in mild measure. A powerful alternative technique with which to eliminate really no-no activities (which every dog will do from time to time) is to encourage some competing activity that is incompatible with performance of the undesirable one. Technically referred to as "response-substitution training," it has a wealth of applications in everyday living. For instance, the dog that attacks visitors at the door need not be punished for showing a territorial reaction, but instead be trained to sit or lie in the hall, probably near to the door, and await some suitable reward. Experienced dog trainers will recognize this concept from use of the "down" signal, which has been traditionally used to block dogs from such dangers as running after other animals or into traffic. There are countless other applications of the response-substitution technique in canine therapy to overcome problem behaviors, for which see Part Three.

*Mimicry: copycat dogs.* The idea of a dog actually copying its master may seem a little farfetched, but (believe me) dogs often do attempt to reproduce human situations and postures. How many times do you lie or sit and then find that your dog lies or sits beside you? My setter Sam immediately occupies the driver's seat when I leave him alone in the car; his howling is reliably precipitated by our singing; he runs when I run, swims, sleeps and more; he is an Irish mimic! More to the point, one dog can be a very good instructor of another in performing complex tasks. It is traditional among farmers to "run on" a puppy with its mother, where she seems to school it in the skills of shepherding. Some farmers even tie the pupil to its trainer dog with a short length of string, though that is not a procedure I would recommend. Certainly in an applied context such as sniffer dogs seeking drugs or explosives, an experienced "instructor dog" can dramatically simplify the training process.

Springer spaniels are often used for drug and explosive detection work because they express an endless enthusiasm, tireless energy and a hunger for play. During a recent trip to Iceland, I witnessed a pack of thirteen English springers "working" for an object we had hidden in an overgrown hay field some 200 meters from home. They fanned out in twos and threes, then came together when a trio was successful in locating the trophy. The trainer, John Gudjonsson, then nicely demonstrated how each of his dogs could perform the same task alone. Originally, all his dogs were "trained" by a matriarchal dog whom John had himself trained using traditional methods. As is well known, "mother does know best," and John was realistic enough to recognize that dogs are more expert about canine behavior than we humans. Unfortunately, the way that modern puppies are weaned early and then dispatched to dog-free homes destroys this natural system of canine apprenticeships.

*Head control.* Canine halters were originally devised simply to stop dogs pulling, but I quickly realized that it had a wealth of other applications for solving canine problems. It greatly simplifies training because it permits you to guide the dog into precisely the posture or place that you want him to be in. Without a halter you are liable to end up pushing, shoving and prodding the poor dog, using too much force for either of you. The idea of using halters in this role is somewhat like that of Colonel Most and his induction method, except that control is achieved by fingertip pressure rather than by bulging biceps.

The linkage of head control to instrumental learning is quite practical and can considerably speed up the training of unusual activities. Let us take a completely untrained dog that never spontaneously lies down in a neat position, but always flops languorously over to one side. To improve upon this dog's "down" response, position it correctly with the halter, then reward just as it takes up the appropriate posture.

Halters such as the Halti and Promise collar are especially useful in training dogs to run agility courses, which is also best done by copying another experienced dog. Have the trainee dog wear the headcollar and lead it along the course, giving each activity a verbal label before, during and after successful performance on each item of apparatus.

Most simple of all is training a persistently pulling dog to walk and heel with a halter. This is dealt with in the next chapter, the theory being that as the dog moves just parallel to you, you administer the "heel" command, which word quickly assumes instrumental control over the dog walking alongside its owner.

It is the combination of instrumental learning, mimicry and accurate head control which provides the key elements for dog training the Mugford way. It can all be done so effortlessly and give such pleasure that the challenge is now only to our imagination that must dream up new things for a dog to learn. They do have to sit, stay, come and heel, but that alone will hardly make you a worthy companion to your canine friend or sufficiently stretch his intelligence.

Read on!

Part Two

# THE PRACTICE OF
# DOG TRAINING

# 6
# Adult Education:
## *Training Useful Behaviors*

Old dogs really do learn new tricks and there is no reason why your occasionally chaotic canine cannot pick up the accepted rules of obedience. Let's assume that you are one of the millions of owners who have peeped into a traditional training club and been amazed at the cacophony of barking and shouting and the sight of dogs being hurled about on choke chains. Maybe you decided that you would rather have an untrained dog! But maybe your dog occasionally shows you up in public: he won't come back when you want him, he sits beside the table begging for food, he pulls on the leash and has a habit of wiping his paws on the seat of women's dresses. If only, if only you had trained him!

The good news is that old dogs can very easily learn new tricks if you go about it in the correct way. It's up to you, the owner, to pick and choose the appropriate menu for your particular dog from both the nouvelle cuisine and the more traditional methods described in this book. The two essential things to remember are that you must have a consistently calm attitude and you must never shout at your dog, and certainly never say No!

I have one other inflexible rule, which concerns the choke chain that someone may try to persuade you to hang on your best friend's neck.

Please do not obey a choke-trainer, and if you already possess a chain throw it away—otherwise you had better throw away this book, because the pain of a choker will undo any possible good you may find in the pages to follow.

The practice of training dogs has become synonymous with sharp, spoken commands like Come!, Sit!, Stay! or Dowwwn! It need not be so, and hand signals have definite advantages, either alone or in combination with speech. As was mentioned earlier, deaf dogs can be trained to a high standard using hand signals of the type shown in the photos. Other dogs are better trained using a whistle, and the gundog fraternity has a code which works as well in the house as on the hunt. What matters is to choose the medium that the dog attends to, and thereafter to keep the message consistently simple. For instance, if the right hand is used to signal "down," don't occasionally use the left which is associated with the "sit" posture. Dogs are cleverer than most of us imagine, and they do spot the minor deviation. If you encounter difficulties in training, it is probably your mistake rather than his. It is more likely that the dog wants to please rather than to embarrass you, so go easy on him.


## RECALL: RETURNING TO A FRIEND

It is the easiest thing in the world to train a dog to come when you have him or her from a puppy, but it might get harder when you are in competition with the smells of rabbits, the sight of another dog, or the attraction of the neighbor's cat. Be sure that, occasionally, every dog lets its owner down. What you can do, though, is to improve the probability or chances of his returning when you want him to.

Your first objective should be to utilize the dog's name or some other arousing stimulus to focus his attention on you. The contact call or signal is the spoken word "Come," supplemented by a hand signal (arms apart and horizontal, palms facing the dog, slightly crouched) and the payoff of your company, your tender hands, maybe a tidbit. The whistle signal is beep-beep-beep-beep, repeatedly.

There are bound to be occasions when your dog comes to you spontaneously: to smell your feet, to lick your face or to solicit play. Watch out for these movements, and as he arrives within a two- to three-meter range, say "Come" and/or give the matching hand signal. When he arrives, share in a joyful reunion, massage him on the spots

he likes and sometimes give him a tidbit (i.e., an intermittent reinforcement schedule). By this process, you will instrumentally condition a strong response to the "come" signal. Continue this investment
until he reliably comes in your house and garden. Now you are ready
for the outdoor test.

Go to the middle of a wilderness area, away from the distractions of
traffic, people or dogs. Alternatively, choose an enclosed space such as
a tennis court or a local park where the gates are closed. Have your
dog on an extending leash or long rope and repeat the instrumental
sequence described above: when he spontaneously returns to you
deliver the signal "Come." Now obtain his attention by calling his
name, by rattling a tin can, by an ultrasonic beam, heavy breathing, a
strained-intensity scream, or whatever else it takes! Maybe you will
have to act like a bird with a broken wing, emit the puppy whine or
run away. As he returns, give your "come" signal and prepare the
reward, consistently on the first few occasions but thereafter only
intermittently.

Just occasionally, you will have a dog, probably an Afghan or an
Irish setter, who really does not care what you do to try to attract his
attention. For him, the joy of running exceeds any possible distraction
or payoff that you could offer. For such dogs you might have to resort
to the traditional classical conditioning method, but before taking this
desperate measure, you should have invested several weeks in the
instrumental program described here.

This is how to train a persistent runaway dog. With your extending
leash or long line attached to his collar, call his name, give the command, then throw a rattly tin can (see page 114) just beyond him.
Crouch down to ground level and invite him in, forcefully if necessary.
Repeat and repeat. The "Come" command then becomes a safety
signal for avoidance of the unpleasant sound of the rattling can, or the
humiliation of being dragged toward you. We are here resorting to
the traditional dog trainers' stock in trade, compulsion, which neither
you, I, nor your dog will be happy with: let's hope it won't be needed.

## HEEL!: MY FRIEND AND I TOGETHER

Traditional training has made more of a fuss of getting dogs to heel
than of any other aspect of canine behavior. Dogs are so often trau-
matized with chains, sticks and verbal abuse; they are thrown around

on slippery floors and generally made to have a miserable time. A more ethological approach makes it all seem like child's play. Any and every dog will heel with a combination of the methods outlined below, and it should all be achieved in a matter of minutes.

First let's look at the natural walking-loping gait of the wolf and dog. They can maintain a comfortable speed of 5–6 mph (11 km/hr), for eight to fifteen hours a day. Our natural human walking speed varies between 1 mph and 3 mph, and only the exceptionally athletic type will want to walk at 5 mph. That is the first obstacle to a dog walking beside you: you are probably too slow for him. In heel training we are seeking a proximity response. The aim is for the dog to walk near to you rather than ahead, behind or to the side. The reason why dogs traditionally walk on your left is that cavalrymen used to walk horses on their left but carry a rifle in their right hand. Rifles are not nowadays needed to walk the dog!

Many people find that their dog heels better off the leash than on. Restraint induces so-called barrier behaviors in a dog; just as a confined zoo animal paces fruitlessly to and fro to seek escape from its cage, so dogs tend to pull at the end of their leash. The answer is to make the leash seemingly endless, by using an extending leash. Everybody gets in a tangle with extending leashes at first, but it's not difficult to learn how to use them.

Attach the buckle of the leash to a fixed object such as a post. Swing your fully extended arms up and down, as though you were walking at a comfortable loping gait. On the second or third downward swing of your left hand, lightly press the brake button. You will produce a click from within the case of the extending leash. This sound can be the orientating signal for subsequent heel work and make the spoken command unnecessary.

For many puppies and dogs that is all one needs: an extending leash attached to a flat collar. Why a flat collar rather than, say, a round collar or a choke chain? Readers will understand my aversion to the choke chain, but my policy on the width of collars is that they should extend over at least two cervical vertebrae; in a Labrador-proportioned dog that might mean a one-inch (25 mm) collar. A fixed collar provides a definite tactile sensation for the dog, nicely accompanying the click action of the extending leash. The gradual choking action of a chain or a slack collar gives a diffuse sensation which does not provide such a precise discriminative stimulus. The intention is not to yank the dog back using the leash–collar combination, but to send a message lightly down the leash that you want the dog to resume the proximity response of "heel" beside you. The signal for proximity should be the word "heel" itself, possibly a pat of your thigh with the flat of your free right hand or with the case of the extending leash in your left hand. Please note that the leash is not held across your body in the traditional dog-training manner; an extending leash makes the double-handed approach redundant and frees your right hand to do something better.

If your dog ignores the "heel" signal, speed up your walking and when he naturally arrives beside your body, at precisely the desired position, say "Heel" and reward his closeness with soft, sweet talk, a touch of your hand or sometimes a tidbit. You see many dogs at shows parading around the ring gazing up at their owners who have a little food secreted between their fingers, behind an ear or even in their mouth. That can become a tiresome appeal to the dog's gluttony rather than exploitation of a naturally attentive and affectionate relationship between man and dog.

Unfortunately, there are a few dogs that will not respond to the above learning regime, or there are those whose strength and body weight always gives them the advantage over a frail owner. Do not despair; you still need not resort to chains or spiked collars and cruelty. It is for these people that I invented the Halti, the halter that makes walking the dog as simple as a stroll in the park. Indeed, the idea of the Halti was originally born out of the misfortune of my having a chronic back problem which was made worse by having to treat big, powerful, aggressive dogs. This was in November 1984. I had been called in to treat a gigantic Irish wolfhound with a tendency to consume other people's small white dogs. My wife Vivienne and I happened upon the combination of straps that created a perfect steering device for dogs, just as larger halters are used on horses. A million or two Haltis later, I can say that this device has been the answer to many dog owners' prayers, but it is usually used as a passive rather than as an active technique for training dogs to heel. But that need not be so, and dogs can learn a great deal while wearing a halter.

When first fitted, some dogs struggle and object to the Halti, but most accept it within minutes. There are different strategies to overcome any initial discomfort, my favorite being to distract the dog, keep it running, playing, fixated upon food and too busy to worry about the halter. The way to do it is to start by fitting the halter alone—not attached to a leash. Then attach an extending leash and continue running, joking and giving the dog tidbits until his pawing stops. Always use the lightest touch, holding a long line or extending leash in your left hand to guide the dog's head gently to the right. The leash should dangle slack and free beneath the dog's right side. Never jerk a dog's neck back: It is not dangerous to do so, but it is unkind and unnecessary. In tests at the Animal Behaviour Centre, we have found that the intensity of a dog's pull on the collar is reduced from a factor of 250 percent of its body weight to less than 1 percent. The most diminutive person can now safely lead the most powerful dog. Just a few owners complain that the dog is still able to pull on the Halti, and the reason is always that the dog has learned to stiffen its neck muscles and make the head an extension of the body. We call this the head-down position, a classic solution sometimes devised by resourceful dogs like Dobermans. The technique to overcome it is to let the dog run ahead on its extending leash and then very lightly click the leash and gently tug to the right. By then the dog will have relaxed his muscles so that he becomes susceptible to the sideways-steering pull of the halter.

Dogs can be obliged to heel on a halter in a passive way and later be trained by the instrumental method described earlier. Alternatively, the halter can be worn loose on the dog's head with the leash attached to an ordinary collar. Finally, a few wily dogs learn to heel without even wearing a halter: the owner just has to carry the halter as a symbolic threat, in case the dog does not adopt the desired heel position.

Do remember that to walk at a slow speed in a regulated position is unnatural behavior for dogs. Only demand the strict heel position for as long as is necessary, and at other times permit them to stop, sniff, stray forward or explore to back and side. After all, your dog is not in the army, and whose walk is it anyway?

## SIT: PLACE BUTTOCKS COMFORTABLY

Every dog will occasionally sit; it's a naturally comfortable position for them to adopt. It is also the easiest position to train using either classical or instrumental procedures. The classical approach is to press the dog's buttocks down while at the same time lifting the dog's neck upward, saying "Sittt!" as the dog's bottom sinks toward *terra firma*. Again, it seems extraordinary to me that this combination of force and pain is applied by so many trainers to create an action that young and old dogs spontaneously perform anyway.

The instrumental approach is outlined in Chapter 3; the procedure in more detail is as follows. Wait and watch your dog until he sits in what you believe to be the appropriate folding of paws and legs. At that moment say "Sit" quietly, then walk over and pat or tidbit-reward him. By approaching him, you may have inadvertently triggered your dog to lie down. It is natural for a dog to unfold and relax when praised and happy, so don't punish him when he goes down when you wanted him to sit. Just withdraw, distract the dog to stand or to follow you and then wait for him to sit again, and repeat. Good timing is all that is required for a 100 percent success rate. New puppy-owners should succeed in training "sit" within the first day of acquiring their six-week-old puppy; it may take a little longer with an adult but not much longer.

The hand signal for "sit" is simple. Partially raise, then part lower the left hand with palm facing the dog. Some adult dogs are never taught to sit as a matter of policy: for instance the show fraternity often prefer their dogs to stand. If you come by a rehomed show dog, you can speed up the instrumental approach by exploiting the Halti system. That is, occasionally lift the dog's head on a halter, and the dog's buttocks will naturally go down. The moment his bottom touches ground, say "Sit," then reward as before. This is not a derivative of the traditional dog-training "sit" method, which is to give the command before rather than after the dog adopts the desired posture. Most dogs willingly sit for food, but an overreliance on food as a reinforcement system for training "sit" can be a disadvantage: he may learn to perform at the table but not at the curb.

## DOWN: LET TENSE LEGS UNFOLD

You will find many more harsh methods in other dog training books on how to get a dog to lie down on command. There is really no need, because like "sit," "down" is an easily conditioned instrumental response. The traditional approach is to strangulate the poor dog as the trainer's foot engages the choke chain and pushes it to the ground. Many a dog will panic, struggle, possibly bite its trainer (serves them right!) and certainly be reluctant to permit touching or training in the same context. You would do better to proceed as follows.

Go for a jog, taking the dog with you to the point of his being weary. Stop, and the dog will hopefully lie down in exhaustion. At that moment, say "down," then reward with a tidbit or praise. Continue your run, and repeat. Note the command is given after rather than before the animal voluntarily adopted the desired position. Later, you may wish to refine the "down" posture so that a fairly precise posture is required to earn the payoff: perhaps you want your dog in the classic sphinx position, more decorous than a sprawled-out, legs-akimbo state. Of course, dogs do not just lie down because they are exhausted after a jog, and the instrumental method can be applied to dogs at any age and for any reason that they might lie in a prone position. The hand signal for "down" is an exaggeration of that for "sit." Swing the right hand to vertical, then lower as the dog itself drops to the ground. As the dog's proficiency at "down" improves, the hand signal can be abbreviated to something more simple, like the still, horizontal hold of your hand. The whistle command for "down" is a single, short blast.

There is one other method which is sometimes recommended as a humane alternative to the traditionally compulsive technique mentioned earlier. That is to take a tidbit, hold it in your hand and near to the dog's mouth, then bring it down his chest, hoping he will follow it and fall into the desired posture. However, in the approach that is usually used by trainers, the "down" command precedes rather than follows adoption of the desired posture. I really would not recommend this because the "down" response then becomes cued to your possession of a tidbit, which may not always be convenient. The instrumental approach I have described for training "down" wins over other methods because it is more humane and more efficient.

## STAY: FREEZE!

It is useful to have a dog stay where you want him to be without resorting to some form of canine pin-down. Again, the instrumental procedure is our method of choice. It must be understood that the "stay" command can only follow performance of some other instrumentally conditioned task. For instance, you may have brought the "sit" response under instrumental control, and can delay reward for a period which is labeled by the signal "stay" or "wait." Then you can introduce intervals of increasing duration between the "sit" command and the terminal reward for obeying "stay" or "wait."

The word "wait" would be usefully repeated at three- to five-second intervals in the early stages of training, coupled with the flat-of-hand signal while staring directly into the dog's eyes. Very soon, the word "wait" will itself acquire powerful secondary reinforcing properties: it need not always be a cue for imminent reward. We can now extend the "wait" concept to performance of other behaviors, such as "down" before offering food, and so on.

A common difficulty in training is the manner chosen to terminate the "stay" command. Some prefer to make a distinction between "wait" and "stay," seeing "wait" as a temporary immobility from which the dog can be removed by a "come" command, whereas "stay" requires the physical return of the trainer to the dog. However, I have never found the distinction between stay and wait to be important: most dogs seem able to rely upon the friendly administration of a "come" command to terminate either situation at any distance.

## FETCH–RETRIEVE: CHASE, KILL, SHARE

Chase–kill behavior is fundamental to the survival of a hunting carnivore such as the wolf, and provides the basis for retrieval by dogs. It is a useful activity to develop as it saves humans having to bend down and pick up objects fallen to dog level. It is also a key element in most games of object play, and is particularly exaggerated in the herding breeds of dogs.

The tendency to hold and carry objects has also been genetically modified—exaggerated in breeds like golden retrievers and Labradors, but less common in terriers. Retrieval behavior is part of the food-carrying care system where adult wolves transport parts of a kill back to the puppies, so it is an intensely social and even altruistic activity. I sometimes wonder whether it is worth attempting to train retrieval behavior if it is not spontaneously exhibited by a dog during normal play. It probably is not and if you want a retriever, you should buy a retriever! However, assuming your dog does have a natural tendency to chase, collect and hold, here is how it can be instrumentally managed.

Take your dog's favorite toy and keep it from him for a few hours so that it becomes more valued by its absence. Attach it to a thin string about thirty to fifty feet. Put your dog into a sit position, and "stay." Throw the toy and point him in the right direction with your hand. Then, release your dog from the stay and as he chases toward the toy say "Fetch." As he picks it up say "Hold." Let him do a few circuits with it, keeping the cord slack so that it does not become a tug-of-war. Eventually, use the "come" command, and as he approaches you while holding the toy, say "Bring." When he comes close enough to touch, praise and reward him. If he voluntarily drops the object, say or indicate "drop" but be sure to have a tidbit to give. The act of offering a food reward should oblige him to drop the object because there is competition between incompatible actions.

The successful and trouble-free development of a good retrieve sequence depends upon the dog's having a natural predatory interest in toys and your having first trained him to sit–stay–come. It is important that these are well-developed before formalizing the rules of object retrieval. Once trained on the dog's favorite toy, you can progress to a variety of other objects when each can be labeled with its name. Thus, "fetch the shoe," "fetch the ball," the squeaky toy, etc.

Jess was an early patient of mine who opened my mind to the learning ability of dogs. He was a collie cross, having a remarkable object-memory of ninety-plus items to which more were constantly being added. His mistress had had an entertaining time training and building upon Jess's natural retrieve tendencies by labeling any number of household objects which Jess could both find and return to their original locations. Assistance dogs perform a similar task for physically handicapped people, picking up those hard-to-reach objects around the home. But I repeat, if your dog does not want to do this I do not believe it is ethical to force him. The function of dog training is to channel and develop natural or existing response tendencies, not to impose new and unnatural actions.

## To Bark or Not to Bark

Most dogs bark; even basenjis make a sort of yodel. Barking can be easily brought under external control by instrumental techniques. A puppy or dog will spontaneously bark, usually to a knock at the door, possibly during the excitement of a wind-up game or when hunting. On hearing that first bark, literally the first bark you hear, say "Speak," then praise and reward the dog. For several weeks repeat the procedure constantly: the dog barks, you say "Speak," and he receives a payoff. Soon you should have his barking under instrumental control: you say "Speak," and he will bark, whereas he will be less likely to bark without the command. This approach is a kind way of solving nuisance barking, by the owner formally directing it.

A similar rationale can apply to howling (singing): it is the natural contact call between members of a dog pack. Howling is normally a dawn or dusk behavior before the pack departs and when the wolves return from a hunt. It can have interesting musical qualities and dogs seem to enjoy participating in the performance, my setter Sam being a prime example. The first occasion on which Sam spontaneously demonstrated his singing ability was at my daughter's fourth birthday party, when we sang "Happy Birthday, Ruth." His behavior was subsequently conditioned to our holding our heads back with lips in an "O" shape: the original stimulus of singing children is no longer necessary. Sam is now an established performer on nationwide radio and TV, including musical request shows!

Although it is an amazing party trick to have a dog whine to the signal "sad," bark to "speak," or growl to "angry," there is a more serious side to bringing vocalizations of a dog under instrumental control. Having the power to invoke silence is certainly going to please your neighbors, and in these violent times it is also good to have a dog with a vocal repertoire that can impress would-be burglars.

## TRACKING: USING YOUR NOSE

When hunting, wolves utilize all their senses for locating prey, but at a distance they rely heavily upon their sense of smell. The olfactory sense has been somewhat reduced by the process of domestication, but all breeds of dogs still have an impressive acuity and discrimination ability for smells. Unfortunately, the world of humans, especially in our cities, is dramatically polluted with competing olfactory information, making it difficult for an urban dog to gain much experience of tracking. Instead, reserve such pleasures for trips to the country where pristine acres unsullied by the soles and pads of other canines and humans can be found.

The dog-tracking fraternity are a group of enthusiasts who take the subject very seriously, awarding one another quaintly pretentious qualifications and their dogs titles such as TDex! There are amazingly complicated and boring training manuals solely devoted to the subject. But you and I are into dogs for enjoyment, so I will describe only the fun approach to scent training here.

Take a dog who likes his food, and at feeding time drag his bowl on a straight line across the lawn or field for fifty to two hundred feet. Let him see what you have done and point him in the right direction. When released, he will naturally chase after the track, relying on visual more than olfactory cues. On subsequent days, make things more complicated by walking through longer grass and increasing the distance, eventually preventing him from watching the course you have taken. Always keep the task success-orientated so that you are rewarding good behavior rather than coping with the frustration of failure. Next add first one bend, then a second and more bends to the track. Eventually, lift up the bowl so that it is just your footprints the dog is following, not the bowl itself.

The approach described here is the so-called free-tracking method. It can be easily extended to object retrieval, joining the tracking sequence to fetch–retrieve as described earlier. Finally, it is sensible to set the dog off on a track with an unusual form of words, such as "go find," or he will take himself off on perpetual "autotrack" to roam in search of the setting sun and your footprints.

But you don't have to be out in the woods to have fun with your dog tracking. It can be done at home or in the garden, hiding suitably scented objects under carpets, behind furniture or shrubs, just triggered by the command "go find." Life can be so boring for the dog of today; what better than to stretch his object memory and make him work with his nose?

## ELIMINATION: BOWEL AND BLADDER CONTROL

We humans tend to suffer anxiety attacks at the thought of our dog depositing urine and feces in the wrong place and at the wrong time: always better in someone else's backyard or when no one is looking! To avoided such unpleasantness, it is as well to take control of your dog's eliminatory activities. The topic will be covered later, in Chapter 14, but even the best-behaved dog can be an embarrassment if he flouts our human rules about what is permissible. This is the way to take instrumental control of your dog's bladder and bowel.

Walk your dog so that you are always reasonably close together.

That probably means restraining him on an extending leash or with you in the garden, rather than running free over large areas. At each and every urination, devise some special word such as "wee wee," "shhhh," etc. (Be wildly original here!) Just say it when he has performed, then reward him with praise, a brief period of tug play or even a tidbit. Your dog will defecate less frequently than he urinates, on average 2.7 times per day. When that happens, say the chosen word, beginning just as your dog circles, sniffs and adopts the crouch posture that is characteristic of defecation. This word could perhaps be the name of an esteemed family member or of your favorite politician. In no time, Uncle Mort or Mr. Smith will be the verbal cue on which your dog will excrete when it suits you.

You might also want to direct your dog to a particular spot to defecate. He is least likely to want to perform in the place where he is fed. So, move his food bowl to each of the spots on the lawn where he has defecated. After that take him to the spot where you do wish him to go, perhaps down by the compost heap, out of sight of the house. Wait, watch and again reward him for having used the appointed spot.

Because of the significant marking or communicatory component to both urination and defecation in dogs, it may be wise to import a freshly produced bolus from a dog known to your pet, together with a tinkle of his or her urine, and put them on the midden-to-be. In practice, it is probably easier to import Fido's best friend to deposit it for you rather than bringing it home in your handbag. There will be some difficulty in toilet training if your dog was punished when a puppy. That is why house-training puppies should always be conducted by the most indulgent and calm of procedures, as described in Chapter 14.


## Tricks: Amazing Stunts

Personally, I do not like animals performing unnatural acts either commercially on film, in a circus or at someone's home. Nevertheless, dogs like to please and my high-minded philosophical objections can probably not always be sustained on objective animal welfare grounds.

So you want your dog to perform amazing feats which will impress the neighbors and family. How do you go about it? Some important theoretical notions are needed if you are to succeed. First, you need to know all about "chaining" (see Chapter 5), where you break down a complex task into small, easily performed components, arranged in a logical order. Having established the activity you want the dog to perform, your aim should be to achieve partial performance and then shape or move the behavior toward that final objective.

For instance, maybe you want your dog to jump through hoops. Begin by having a very large hoop that you can walk through and invite your dog to mimic and follow. Make the hoop smaller and smaller in stages, perhaps by using a coiled piece of polyethylene pipe. Finally, you will end up with a hoop just the right size for your dog to jump through. Reward at each stage of the training regime, which could well be completed in as few as one or two days. Later, move the hoop off the ground, a few inches at a time. Always work at a speed and for a time which maintains your dog's interest; he must never become bored. Finally, you will be able to hold the hoop at any level, in a variety of positions and at any place. You have made your debut as a professional animal trainer!

Another essential concept for training tricks has already been mentioned in this book: exploitation of existing response tendencies or quirks, and developing them by instrumental techniques. For instance, many dogs have a habit of rolling over to display their belly (an inguinal display): this can be a sign of fear, an attempt to divert aggression, even an act of sexual invitation. You can condition the inguinal display to the word "dead," producing a convincing Hollywoodlike roll-over and collapse of Lassie facing the Mafia. It would be difficult to force a dog to roll over—it's better to wait for his spontaneous performance, then link it to the word "dead" and reward. Once instrumental control of the behavior has been obtained you can speed up the rate of performance by requiring an immediate response and by not rewarding slower ones. Later, double or triple bodyrolls may be demanded before the payoff.

A response easily performed by many small dogs is to beg: sitting on the hindquarters. Some dogs, especially Jack Russells, are sufficiently athletic to do this for minutes and longer at a time, though in others with less robust bodies, many dachshunds for example, it may be physically harmful to adopt such a posture. Again, the behavior of balancing on hind legs has to be part of the dog's spontaneous repertoire before instrumental training should be attempted.

A host of other quaint actions can be tempted out of your dog: lifting a paw to carry a basket or an attaché case, opening cupboards or communicating in a succession of barks, grunts and whines. If you have the time, your dog definitely has the ability.

# 7

# Puppy Care:
## *The Twenty-week Training System*

You are the luckiest person in the world because you have the time, space, imagination and generosity of spirit to take on a puppy. Let's suppose that all the family discussions and arguments have taken place and you have narrowed down the choice to a particular breed and sex. If there are any uncertainties about the wisdom of this decision, you will have talked to your vet, who can act in the role of devil's advocate to warn you off breeds known for their incidence of hereditary defects and management problems. The vet may have recommended a particular breeder, who has a dog about to produce, and you are in her Category A customer list. You like the breeder and she is happy for you to visit at any time, to join her in raising the perfect dog for you.

What follows is an idealized twenty-week system of training and care which will give your puppy the best possible start in life, and which also offers you and the breeder the privileged opportunity to participate in the molding of a life. Mundane realities may prevent you from achieving all of these objectives, but compromises can be made, and times to achieve particular goals can be brought forward or delayed. All that matters is that you try to do your best for this new life.

## WEEK 1

You are not a canine midwife so let's hope that birth was uneventful and a litter of well-formed pups have warmth, a conscientious mother and an ample milk supply. There may have been discussion about whether or not to allow all the puppies to live. On the one hand tender humanity says that each puppy should be allowed life, but on the other, one has to ask whether the mother can produce sufficient milk and maternal energies to raise all her puppies. Another consideration about culling is the financial reality that each puppy is a potential sale for the breeder. In my view, the routine culling of litters down to some moderate and manageable number of, say, six puppies, cannot be justified on either welfare or even practical behavioral grounds. There are admirable food supplements available for puppies nowadays, and what really matters is the overall quality of maternal care. For instance, does the mother reliably stimulate urogenital reflexes and sensory development of her puppies? Is she an ever-present safety net who can prevent them from straying from the nest, and is her overall temperament a good model for the puppies to emulate?

By the third day after the birth, the relationship of the mother to her puppies should be a secure and confident one and she should seem positively to invite attention by humans whom she knows. You are a stranger and it may be threatening and inappropriate for you to become much involved with the puppies now, so be content with a distant look. The breeder and other members of her family should examine each of the puppies at this stage, checking that there are no infections of the umbilicus, and no other obvious abnormalities requiring veterinary attention. This should be done on a twice-daily basis, remembering that the dog is a social animal for whom the presence of puppies becomes an event for participation by the whole pack; motherhood in wild canids is not a private affair, nor should it be for domestic dogs!

## WEEK 2

By day seven the crawling reflexes of the puppies are well-formed and they can usually right themselves if turned over. The puppies' vocalizations are characteristically loud and evoke strong interest from the mother. Their eyes are still closed and will remain so until the eighth to tenth day. The puppy cries whenever its position is changed, such as when lifted, handled or examined by the breeder. Nevertheless, this is what should be done in the second week, two to five minutes devoted to gentling and handling each pup when the mother is away at her food or being exercised. This handling process teaches the pups to distinguish textures, and the just-functional olfactory system will pick up human smells that may assist in the later bonding process. In general, the first two weeks of puppies' lives belong to the mother; she is their best caretaker and humans usually need only be supportive aunts. Like members of a wolf pack, our role is to offer food and security.

## WEEK 3

This is the time that you, the prospective owner, can help development of your puppy-to-be. He has left the neonatal stage of development when the central nervous system was rapidly developing in both its form and function. It is at this time, the beginning of what is sometimes referred to as the transitional period, that puppies gradually develop the potential to see and hear, adding to their already well-developed senses of touch, taste and smell.

By the end of the third week, some wobbly walking may take place and you might now volunteer to the breeder your willingness to join in with handling the puppies. No scientific studies exist to determine what is an optimum period for handling, nor its quality and quantity. I suggest three to four occasions per day, each of about two to three minutes per puppy. Gentle the puppy by holding him in your hands and stroking all parts of his body; roll him over and place him on the floor to experience different surfaces. Talk to him softly and constantly.

There are ample studies on kittens and human babies to indicate that environmental restriction of infants at this stage can have disastrous effects upon development of the visual cortex and other sensory systems later on in life. The additional sensations that come from handling help to develop the sensory and neurological competence of puppies.

The three-week-old puppy is gradually forming a visual image of humans as a source of positive experiences and useful resources to whom it can pleasurably relate. You might put into practice the theory of olfactory imprinting by exposing the young puppy to your own underarm sweaty smells. You will note the mother's continuing conscientious evocation of the urinatory–defecatory reflex by licking her pups on their lower abdomens, and you can stimulate the same urinatory reflex in the third week by gently stroking them in the genital region with a finger. As the puppy urinates, state the word you propose to utilize throughout life. For the Mugford dogs, the word "busy" has been chosen because it is unusual and it is not often used in other contexts. Do not, even at this stage, confuse the puppy with "good boy" or "good girl" after performing this reflex evacuation.

## WEEK 4

Your puppy is now well on the way to becoming a dog. It can hopefully walk a few feet or more outside the nest and shows interest in following his litter mates and mother. This is the time to begin discussing with the breeder which might be the best puppy for you. The size, behavior and general character of puppies are usually rather similar, much more highly correlated within litters than between litters. So don't worry greatly about which puppy: it would be an arbitrary decision with only a veneer of scientific justification to imagine that one puppy is more forward and "intelligent" than another. Believe that every puppy has the potential to become a remarkable dog, and it probably will.

Continue to lift the puppy from the nest for the same handling exercises as in earlier weeks. Take him outside the nest area, onto carpets, concrete and other surfaces which offer a secure grip. Do not place him on shiny floors such as vinyl, which make it difficult for him to right himself and gain a footing. With no other distractions in the room, get down on hands and knees and walk away, encouraging him to follow. Even at this stage say "Come, come!" If you are sure that this is the puppy for you, start thinking of a name and present it to the family for democratic debate. With our latest setter puppy, the choice was between Neurone (my favorite) and Apollo from my daughters. Naturally, the girls' choice prevailed, and his friends call him Pollo!

Toward the end of the fourth week, puppies will change their oral habits from just sucking and gently mouthing to a definite grasp with the jaws. Offer a little slurried solid food on your finger to be licked, just as it might lick mother's lips when they are tainted with food. Do not expect substantial quantities of solid food to be consumed at this stage, however: mother is still the great provider.

## WEEK 5

By now, your puppy should show a definite interest in people, and might even show a particular liking for regular visitors. Continue the handling exercises, followed by "come" training. When the puppy urinates, even defecates out of the nest, use your special word. Try to reward each supervised urination and defecation with a lick of food from your finger.

Significant quantities of solid food should be taken by the litter as a group, with or without the presence of mother. Some mothers will stand back and defer to their offspring eating; others will seemingly compete with the puppies. In nature, the usual situation is that adult wolves return from a hunt with partially digested meat in their stomachs, which is regurgitated as the puppies pester the adults' lips. This is the biological basis for the tendency of dogs to lick humans around the face and especially around the mouth. Continue to develop the puppies' interest in your hands by occasionally offering food buried within your cupped hands. You then become a part of the maternal care process and feeding is not just a competitive activity between siblings.

By the end of the fifth week, your puppy might show an interest in his name, which you can link to the "come" word when training him to follow. Continue with toilet training by removing the puppy from the nest area indoors and taking him to a spot outdoors sharing the same features as he will later use for excreting as an adult. In the Mugford household, the chosen substrate is a patch of wood chippings; in others it might be grass or concrete. Substrate preferences are learned at this early age, usually by copying or subtle encouragement from the mother.

Conscientious breeders should make a major effort to assist in this process of natural house-training by giving the puppies sufficient space to get away from their nest area. A crowded kennel pen forces puppies passively to soil their environment and it is just not good enough to keep them on a deep litter of shredded newspapers. I would specifically recommend against toilet training by the so-called paper method unless you will be prepared to cover your own garden in mucky, wet newspaper.

By the fifth week, you should really feel that your puppy's personality is unfolding and that he relates to you as an individual. But if you have changed your mind and given your heart to another puppy, don't worry; the puppy-person bond is still barely formed.

## WEEK 6

By the sixth week, the puppy-teeth are beginning to sharpen and lengthen, sometimes causing distress to the mother during suckling. When opportunities allow, she may escape from her puppies, perhaps to a high spot where she's out of their reach but still able to watch over them. In the wild at this stage, she would be taking the puppies on longer forays beyond the den and immediate nest area. Indeed, she may have transferred them to several dens, either carrying them by the scruff or letting them follow. It is natural and desirable that puppies be encouraged to follow humans, and the best human to do this is you, his prospective lifetime partner.

Solid food is becoming an increasingly important resource for the puppy, taking over from mother's milk. The breeder will probably have offered the puppies a variety of foods at this stage, from moistened biscuits to cooked meats and rice as well as milky dishes. A varied diet at this age helps to establish a varied gut flora which will stand the puppy in good stead as a barrier to infection later on in life. Offer a little food on your hand to the puppy by way of greeting, maintaining the expectation that hands are always interesting instruments of kindness.

Note that after exhausting rough-and-tumble play with siblings, your puppy sometimes sits. Now is the time for "sit" training (see page 62). The same is true of lying down: say the magic word. You should also by now have fairly reliable control of his bladder and bowels when you take him to the desired location. Wait patiently, let him sniff and circle, then say the word and reward with effusive praise plus tidbit.

Play with siblings is desirable at this age, but try to transfer some of that interest in subject play to you. Be a "victim" of ambushes, ensuring he has at least a 50 percent success rate in "catching" you. There should definitely be a focus of interest in your face and hands as a result of earlier handling, not just an obsession with feet. Excessive interest in ankles and feet arises because these were the only parts of the human body that a puppy encountered. To avoid such a foot fetish, get down to his level, shrink to the world of puppies and let them lick and pull you, a Gulliver among dwarfs.

## WEEK 7

The breeder may have already been debating with her family about whether they can take much more of the rough-and-tumble fun, endless cleaning and damage to carpets from the growing brood. Some of the puppies are due to be sent to their new homes this week, but you have chosen to leave your puppy with the breeder because he is developing nicely and seems to benefit from continuing contact with mother. For instance, the puppy may watch her licking the cat while basking in sunshine together; could it be that cats are not for chasing? Likewise, the mother avoids walking on flower borders, does not jump in the pond: could these too be appropriate and safe actions for puppy to emulate?

At this stage, toilet training is proceeding well; maybe only one of the puppies occasionally performs in the nest overnight. The mother's milk has almost dried up, but you may be fortunate enough to catch a glimpse of her vomiting food for the puppies when returning from a meal, reminding you that, after all, the wolf lives on in these dogs.

## WEEK 8

The die is cast, and all agree that this is the pup for you. A simple bisyllabic word such as Kaiser, Peter, Benji, Winston or Telstar has been selected: all names having a distinctive first letter. The second syllable can always be dropped later in affectionate usage. The puppy has been starved of food for six hours and an assistant has come to drive the car while you hold the puppy. Keep him preoccupied with play and body contact during the journey, ideally low in the car so that he is not confused by the sight of passing countryside. You would do well to avoid having a puppy vomit at this time, as such a trauma may form the basis of a subsequent phobia about traveling by car (see page 176).

## Day 1

*Welcome home, puppy!* You are conscious that the new puppy has just been wrenched from his mother and remaining littermates, so are prepared to be constantly available for him. You won't shut him alone in a puppy crate or bare kitchen at this time, nor will you worry about whether or not there will be a mark on your precious carpets! This is a social animal, an orphan who must be accompanied for most of the time, twenty-four hours a day. On arrival, take him to the garden and the type of surface on which he was trained to urinate and defecate by the breeder. Use that special word and have food to hand as a reward. Feed him indoors, in the kitchen and in other rooms where you do not wish him to excrete. Then let him sleep, which is needed in frequent, short bouts at this age. On the first day, keep things simple; no casual visitors, and especially no curious children who have been waiting for this moment to play with the new puppy: they will overstimulate him.

So far as possible, you have adhered to exactly the same feeding regime as the breeder established: four meals a day with the last solids at 6 p.m. Stay with the puppy for his first evening; let him sleep on your lap if he wants to while you relax and watch TV. Such close contact is right and normal; there is no logical reason why the puppy should be left in the kitchen away from you. If by some mischance there has been an accident, blame yourself rather than the puppy; clean up with a biological detergent and take him outside to continue the process.

At night, there is no question as to where your puppy should be: in your bedroom! You may have read in dog books from previous eras about the risk that your puppy may forever demand to be in your bedroom in the future, and advising you to establish rules about who sleeps where at the outset and to keep to those rules for life. Bunkum! Until nine or ten weeks of age, severe distress will be caused to any puppy suddenly separated from both canine and human contact. The decision about where he sleeps on a permanent basis can be made at a later stage. So, take puppy on one last trip to the garden and retire together. Of course, different considerations arise if you already have a dog; our puppy Pollo never got to sleep with the Mugfords because he had Sam to cuddle up to on his first few nights.

Where to sleep? It might seem to be delightfully indulgent that puppy sleeps in your bed or even you in his bed, but that would be dangerous should you roll over in sleep. Invest in a crate or basket in which puppy can cuddle up with a soft toy such as a discarded doll. The scientific basis for providing such security for young animals is sound and applies to puppies, to orphaned young rhesus monkeys and certainly to human babies, as was shown years ago by the work of the late British psychiatrist John Bowlby. Witness the cost of not providing contact-comfort for the love-deprived orphans of Romania. We now know that early separation is emotionally damaging to all young animals and that frequent cuddles create robust emotions.

Do not expect a puppy to sleep the full eight hours of his first night—that was not what happened at home with littermates and mother. Expect to be roused by a distressed puppy on the first night. Respond immediately and cuddle him; perhaps take him out for a trip to the garden. You may not get much sleep on this first night home; it is indeed like having a baby.

## Day 2

This is the time to visit the vet for a health check. Remember, veterinary clinics are frequented by sick animals that can harbor infectious diseases, the most worrying being parvovirus, distemper and various gastrointestinal infections. It's a sensible precaution to carry puppy in a large, clean towel, so as to avoid direct contact with the floor, table or other patients at the vet's. Now is the time for discussions about worming and vaccinations, a topic on which the individual veterinary surgeon can advise you better than I can. What you should ask of the vet is the chance to get your puppy out and about with other dogs as early as possible, so request a vaccination regime that will achieve early protection. There is quite a choice of vaccines and differences of opinion among vets as to what is the best approach. Much depends upon the perceived risks of infection in your neighborhood. In rural areas and in towns where a high proportion of the adult dog population is vaccinated, the risks of an unvaccinated puppy contracting distemper are considerably smaller than in less fortunate areas where the disease may be rife.

At the moment of what might be a painful injection, distract your puppy with vigorous roughhousing and a tidbit. After all, you do not want your puppy to grow into the proverbial vet-hating dog! The process of vaccination may induce some physiological upset in the puppy, perhaps diarrhea or a slight increase in temperature but not serious illness. For the first twenty-four to forty-eight hours after vaccination, let him have a calm, undemanding time. Then you can resume the training routines of Week 7, progressing to the words "come (name)," saying "sit" when he sits spontaneously, "down" when he lies down, and so on.

Inevitably, your puppy will stray into dangerous areas and activities: he may have pursued the cat, chewed tassels from a treasured carpet, decapitated a daughter's favorite doll or investigated the theory of electricity. The first consideration with a young puppy must be to remove temptation and danger. These are high-risk times for carpets with loose ends, so remove them. Watch out, too, for electric cables, Chippendale chairs, soft slippers, poisonous plants: there may not be much left of your old home! Substitute desirable and acceptable objects, such as natural rubber toys and soft ropes. It is at this time you will really reap the benefit of having a crate for puppy: save his life, your property and simplify house-training (see page 135).

How do you punish a young puppy? The question is asked too often, yet really there is no one answer except to say as little as possible, and only then after all other options have been tried and failed. Do not imagine that it is "natural" for a mother dog to punish her puppies by shaking their scruffs, tapping their noses or similar such gestures of disapproval. These are fallacies from the old world of dog-lore. Remember that puppies are usually highly sound- and vibration-sensitive, so it may be sufficient just to bang a flat surface with the palm of your hand. For another puppy caught in the act of a terrible crime, thwack a rolled-up newspaper on the table to make a loud noise or throw a rattle tin can (see page 114). For yet another, a light flick of water may be more appropriate. During any such punishments, keep quiet. Adult dogs do not go about growling, barking or reprimanding their puppies, so why should you?

## Week 9

You should by now be having nights free of interruptions from a puppy that is clearly relaxed and settled in your bedroom. You are probably also experiencing only rare indoor accidents now, because puppy goes to the appointed spot outside. Puppy comes when called, he sits, lies down, and is an all-around delight. But this is no time for complacency: you have much more to do and to achieve on behalf of your puppy in this, the midpoint of his socialization period.

Until now, you may have been the main source of human contact for your puppy, but now is the time to share him with others. Have your partner, children and others become involved in the puppy's care and training. School each of these delegate-humans in the terminology you have devised for his training (see Chapter 6) and make sure they are consistent in the giving of rewards.

It is also time to bring other animals into puppy's life, perhaps the neighbor's cat or a relative's (vaccinated) adult dog. Your puppy has been out of contact with dogs for a week, so be cautious in managing this first introduction. If the animal seems to be friendly, let them have fun together. The puppy's skeleton is rapidly growing at this age, so be watchful during play with large or rough adult dogs. Certainly, do not let him crash down stairs or fall onto sharp objects.

Now is the time to start teaching "fetch," because most puppies naturally like to carry objects at this stage, and it is a useful trait in an adult dog. Show an interest in what he carries, then back away while calling "Fetch." He will naturally follow you as you move away: when he gets to you, encourage him to give up the object and immediately reward with more rough-and-tumble play. On the subject of food, continue to accustom puppy to accept tidbits from your hands, so they are still seen as instruments of pleasure in the way that puppies of wild dogs look upon the mother's mouth as the source of vomited food. Hands will always be the best instrument for redirecting the dog's licks and greetings from your face.

## WEEK 10

Your puppy probably amazes everybody by his obedience: is he a dog that has grown up before his time? Not at all, only a dog keen to model his behavior upon humans. That will include walks together, so now is the time to think about puppy's first collar and leash. Buy the lightest possible collar with room and sufficient slack for two fingers *at least*. Do no more than make a big fuss over him if he is distressed and attempts to shake it off.

Continue all the other elements of Week 9 and consider reducing the numbers of meals from four to three if one tends to be rejected. It is good practice to spread meals evenly across the day, say at eight, one and six o'clock.

## Week 11

If you have a vehicle, car journeys can now become a daily occurrence. Ideally they should be of brief duration, and always with something pleasant at the end. Never take a puppy on a journey after a large meal (to avoid nausea). It is time for the first walk away from home, but carry puppy to an area not frequented by dogs: the center of a large field is ideal. Go with friends so that you can play the triangulation "come" game. Let him explore, developing his recognition of animal and plant scents.

Attach the lightest-of-light string leashes to his collar and take him around the home and garden. Never yank, but combine the "come" following training, which is now strongly established in puppy, with the notion of "heel." When he stops, you should stop too, and only initiate further walking after positively inviting him to follow.

## Week 12

Heel training should now be well-established, though you might replace the light string leash with an extending leash (see page 119), using a light touch on the brake button. When continuing to teach heel-work, apply the method given on page 59, interspersed with occasional right-left turns, stop, sit and down, for tidbit rewards or praise. Your puppy will be easily distracted by the presence of other dogs during training, but do not reprimand or restrain him from such contacts. At this age they are a vital part of his growing up.

In Weeks 11 and 12 you might well have made a decision about where you want your dog to sleep in the long term: now is the time to wean him from the bedroom and your nighttime company. However, if you want your dog to continue sleeping in your bedroom, that need not be a problem. Puppy should now withstand separation for increasingly long periods during the day, perhaps for two hours at three months old. You can now gradually resume your social and working life as the puppy becomes more independent, whereas at an earlier age the puppy required your near-constant availability.

## WEEK 13

Lead training should really be coming along well and you are able to do accurate heel work both on and off the leash, though hopefully puppy never stops wagging his tail. You can still boast that you have never reprimanded and certainly never smacked your puppy, but you may have occasionally resorted to throwing a tin can his way! I did it with Pollo when he broke a dish while stealing our cats' food.

Devote a minimum of one hour's quality time to your puppy's training each day, perhaps teaching him how to climb stairs, onto boxes and other elevated surfaces. You have probably decided that you no longer want the puppy to jump up during greeting, so on each occasion he does so, step back and drop a tin can. Then drop to the floor to be on the same level as he and stroke him affectionately.

After a consultation with your vet about vaccination policy, you and your puppy will soon want to join the local dog-walking fraternity, where there will be boisterous play between all manner and sizes of dogs and people. Your house-training may seem to have been too successful, because puppy is reluctant to urinate or defecate outside the appointed area. Postpone action until later, when sexual maturity will stimulate greater interest in both investigating and depositing chemical signals from urine and feces.

## WEEK 14

Join a puppy playgroup if one exists in your area; otherwise stick with the gang in the park. If your puppy shows an aptitude, keep building on his retrieve tendency, using soft objects which can be thrown fair distances for return to you. Do not stimulate an interest in chasing and carrying sticks. Horrible injuries to the throat occur when dogs run into the jagged ends of wood, so large balls and soft, man-made objects are safer. Do encourage frequent recalls for a leash to be attached or removed; alternatively employ a retractable leash-in-collar (see page 120).

Your puppy may have made his first territorial "yip" to a knock at the door. Show appreciation; link it to the speak command (see page 66). However, ensure that visitors bring the pleasures of play and an occasional tidbit, so that people always remain this dog's best buddies.

Visit those long-lost friends who lead the good life in the country. Carry your tin can and interrupt unwanted chase tendencies (see page 188). Employ an extending leash or long line for restraint. Stay a day or longer. Remember, this is the age when wolf cubs would begin to accompany older pack members on perfunctory hunts, and you should be guiding puppy to hunting inanimate objects such as a ball, rather than fur or feathered creatures.

## WEEK 15

People remark that your puppy is fearless, but that fearlessness could pose a danger from cars. When walking in trafficked areas, train your dog to sit at every curb and walk close to hedges and walls; if necessary, be prepared to waive the convention of always walking dogs on the left. If there is a tendency to chase traffic, bikes or skateboarders, suppress it with a rattle can or loud siren. After all, such capers can be a matter of life or death. Otherwise enjoy your dog's company by taking him with you to the store, traveling together on trains, going for trips into and out of town.

Sexual games have probably been a part of your puppy's life from four to six weeks, but now he is getting bigger and his clasps of the cat or your ankles more determined. This is quite normal, even before your puppy starts to lift his leg to urinate. This is training for his later adult behavioral repertoire, though you may decide that you would rather he was without sex. Talk to your vet about the subject early on, because puppies are a better surgical risk for neutering than older dogs. Current research indicates no significant disadvantages to early neutering and no reason why either male or female dogs should be sexually mature prior to the operation (see page 195).

## WEEK 16

Four months is often said to herald the end of the era of socialization, as defined by the American scientists John P. Scott, John L. Fuller and colleagues. This does not mean that social learning suddenly stops at this time, though it is true that the basic framework for social skillfulness should by now have been laid. The four-month-old puppy should exchange coordinated signals with other dogs and also relate to the body language, chemistry, tone of voice and everything else that is human.

Your puppy is now almost half-grown: a voracious eater at his maximum rate of weight gain, requiring at least three meals per day. Continue the practice of having some meals with you sitting close to him, and others where you hold the bowl, so that he does not become possessive over food.

See the vet for the final checkup and third vaccination, and it would be wise to purchase a stock of worming pills, using the specified dosage regime. If the vet pronounces that you have a fit dog, start longer walks, say, one to two miles, where possible choosing soft ground rather than hard pavements. Every such walk should have the extra interest of training to the instrumentally conditioned commands, sit, stay, heel and just occasionally, down. Keep your voice jolly and never shout.

Keep up visits to exotic environments. After all, you want your dog to be exposed to varied stimuli while he is young.

## WEEK 17

You may have decided upon a career choice for your puppy: you want him to retrieve game on shoots, to be a champion swimmer, a sniffer, an amazing finder of missing keys and balls, or just a good ratting terrier. This is the time when you should permit your puppy to display these skills naturally. As has already been said, the simplest way of training either herding or scent work is to mimic a trained adult: a dog whose working skills you admire.

In a male dog, you might occasionally see a flicker of adolescent contrariness, even violence. This is the time of social experimentation, just as it is in teenage children. Ensure that if there is confrontation, you achieve final control or win by using your brain rather than by violence. Sidestep, distract or use the technique of response-substitution training (see page 52) rather than attempting to punish aggressive behavior directly.

A useful way of strengthening your general relationship with a puppy at this age is to begin home dental care: brushing his teeth (see page 129). Make it a daily chore so that puppy is accustomed to your

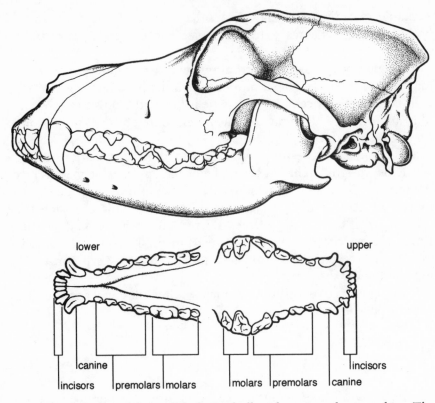

Figure 4. Side view of an adult dog's skull with a normal scissor bite. The plan view of upper and lower jaws shows the ideal layout of the teeth

fingering his mouth. Examine his teeth regularly and check that the adult teeth are developing and taking their proper position along the jaws.

## WEEK 18

Your puppy's nose is beginning to amaze you; perhaps he has just retrieved a tennis ball from the bushes when you thought he had run away and was lost! The olfactory sense of your dog is now finely tuned for scent-work (see page 67). In summer, if there is safe and clean water around, take your puppy swimming. Coordination of limbs for swimming does not come automatically at first, but it is a necessary skill for any adult dog that might accidentally fall into water. It probably comes as a surprise to learn that all dogs cannot instinctively swim; like children they require the opportunity to learn. Breeds differ so much in their reaction to water: Labradors, spaniels and setters find it irresistible, but Dobermans and poodles often hate it. Try, just the same.

Your juvenile puppy may continue to throw tests and challenges your way, but continue in a firm, managerial role. Massage and groom him daily: explore, stroke, hold and tickle him when it seems right to do so, establishing your role as reliable confidant and caretaker.

## WEEK 19

You might now be considering taking up employment again, perhaps on a half-day basis. Note that I regard having a puppy as being incompatible with holding down a full-time job. If you have been routinely leaving your puppy alone for a maximum of two hours without causing undue distress, you could now increase this to four hours. In the future, it is likely you will want to leave your dog occasionally at a boarding kennel, perhaps during vacations or sickness. Accustom your puppy to this experience by taking him to the kennels for one to two hours at first, later for a day or more. This will greatly reduce his distress when boarded as a grown dog and is yet another example of "teach them when they are young."

## WEEK 20

Your puppy is quickly losing his many endearing puppy features and there is the promise of a dog just over the horizon. This is the time when puppy can join in the eccentricities of the lifestyle you propose to share with him from now on: the office, fishing, boating, camping and longer car trips.

As for training, you should now have a dog that does everything you would like him to do, but still has a potential to do much more. Endless tricks are possible, even desirable, if they keep your dog in a constant learning mode.

By now, you can consider reducing his meals to two per day, sometimes requiring that he sit, stay or wait before being offered food. If you have more than one dog, require each to come forward separately by name to avoid possible conflict between them.

If you have children, he will of course already have been in contact with them. However, now is the time when you should know whether you can relax and trust them together, as opposed to maintaining a tense and supervisory eye at all times. It is a sensible rule never to trust young children with a young puppy: matters usually get easier and more predictable from here onward. If in doubt, leave nothing to chance!

At the end of the twenty-week training system, count yourself lucky that you were able to plug into your puppy's early development. In the real world, few of us are so fortunate, because we may have taken on a puppy that has not been through the hands of such a conscientious breeder as yours. All is not lost if your puppy missed out on some of these idealized early experiences: dogs are robust creatures with adaptable ways. What's more, you can adopt the program I have outlined here at any age that suits the circumstances, but always trying to compensate for earlier deprivations if these occurred.

# 8
# The Adopted Dog:
## *Rehome or Rescue*

Some remarkable dogs stray into their owners' lives without a past or a pedigree. The best working sheepdog my father ever owned was Gyp, who chose us and our farm as home by just turning up one wet winter's night. We did the correct thing by contacting local farms, kennels and the police, but no one claimed Gyp. He more than any other kindled my subsequent professional interest in dogs and their ways. He cost my parents not a penny, but heaped rewards on us as an efficient herder, a watchdog and a friend. We were lucky because not all secondhand, rejected, recycled pets are so ideal. How can you reduce the risks of taking on a liability or even a monster in the making? Which is the right dog for you, and which should be avoided? Then again there is the question of settling an adult dog into his new home, training and the like. But first, let's take a consumer's look at adopting a secondhand dog.

### THE STRAY

I seem to be constantly stopping to pick up strays crossing busy roads or scavenging from garbage: it is difficult to turn away from canine down-and-outs. But you should be very cautious indeed before approaching a strange dog and not automatically assume that it is safe to grab him by the collar or scruff. Many dogs in such a situation will be frightened of people, sometimes with good reason. To be effective you must be carrying a leash, or at least a bit of string fashioned into a noose which can be slipped on to give the dog a sense of being under control.

What next? There you are, miles from home with a dog about which you know nothing. Take your time, offer him a tidbit, speak softly and let him check you out. The next priority is to remove yourself and dog from potential danger if you are on a road. Can he be tempted into your car with tidbits? At the first try, leave doors on both sides of the car open, so the dog can see an escape route if frightened.

By now, you should be able to examine the dog for a name tag, which let's hope bears a legible phone number, possibly an address. Failing that, there may be a tattoo: look in his ears and inside hind legs. If the dog bears neither of these forms of identification, there is just a possibility he may carry an electronic tag, for which you will need to contact the local kennel or a veterinarian with the decoder needed to read the implant (see page 123).

Ask people in the area where you found the dog if they recognize him and perhaps know his owner. If you have still drawn a blank, contact the police. They will want information about where you found him, sex of the dog, distinguishing markings, height and so on. After that dogs become available for rehoming, and unfortunately, some for destruction. You can volunteer to keep the dog yourself on the understanding that he will be given up to his owners if they are found. You may find it an emotionally traumatic experience, but to do otherwise would be stealing.


## THE DOGS' HOME

My experience of rescue kennels like Battersea Dogs' Home, National Canine Defence League in Britain and the many SPCAs and Humane Societies throughout North America is that their staff are completely dedicated to the animals, they are often underpaid and always overworked. But it is the kennel staff who know the dog that you may be wanting to adopt, so do seek their help. They will be pleased that you take the time to recognize their professionalism because looks and first impressions are not sensible criteria for selecting your future pet. A few rescue organizations apply formal rules to the behavioral assessment of dogs in their care and attempt to match them to prospective owners. One founder of a private rescue charity, the late Bernard Cuff, didn't even allow prospective adopters to look around his kennels; instead he interviewed them and offered what he believed would be the right dog for them. The worst possible arrangement is to walk along corridors of yapping dogs, jumping up frantically at the doors. It is just too hard on you to have to reject the majority, and you will probably be mistakenly drawn to choosing the most sorry-looking or most hysterical inmate when others would have been more suitable. That is why it is better to be guided by the staff, or by an experienced and objective "doggy" friend who can play the role of devil's advocate.

Having made a preliminary choice, take the dog out of his kennel and apply these simple behavioral tests.

*Approach the dog:* does he tolerate (good), retreat (bad) or show disinterest (neutral)?

*Offer a tidbit on the floor* (taken or rejected).

*Offer a tidbit on your palm* (accepted or rejected).

*Offer your hand to stroke:* is there a friendly response, fear or aggression?

*Take the leash:* is there trust or fear? Take him for a walk outside if possible: does he pull?

*Reactions to dogs:* interest, tolerance, play or aggression. Note the sex of dogs to whom he may react differently.

*Reaction to restraint:* hold each of his paws for a few seconds. Closely examine him, as though for ectoparasites and including his ears. Can you safely hold his muzzle (gently)? Does he object to any part of his body being touched? Try grooming.

*Reaction to a commotion:* have an assistant run past the dog when he is on an extending leash. Does he chase and grab (negative) or just look confused and tolerate (positive)?

*Reactions to other animals:* if it is a rural kennel there may be cats, ducks and any manner of other animals roaming the grounds. Carefully watch the dog's reactions to these animals.

*Reactions to food:* offer a modest amount of palatable food in a bowl, and continue holding the bowl. Is the food taken? Put the bowl down, withdraw, then reapproach and pick up the bowl. Is this tolerated? Warning: if there is any report of food guarding from staff, do not conduct this procedure of repossessing the food bowl. It is a behavioral problem that can be overcome, but you should seriously consider whether this will be the right dog for you, especially if he will be among children.

*Play:* offer a ball, tug toy and the like and try to excite him. Does he go "over the top"? Can you handle his physical strength?

*Reaction to travel:* put him in the car and go for a two-to-three-mile journey. Is he harmonious or a hazard in the car?

Finally, there is that hard-to-define feeling which ultimately determines the bond you will form. Let's call it personality: could you fall in love with this dog? If the dog has passed all these tests and the answer to the personality question is affirmative, take him home.

## BREED RESCUE

To be homeless and available for adoption is not just a prerogative of mongrels. Many thousands of pedigree dogs with good parentage are also out there looking for new owners. The reasons they become available are as many and as varied as the circumstances of people. It may be an Old English sheepdog who just outgrew his owner's home, a dachshund who attacks his littermate brother, a corgi with a desire to kill the family cat, or a dog whose owners have fallen upon hard times and lost their home. Do not necessarily assume that such dogs are all abused and present behavioral problems. The dog's former owners will be as distressed at losing their pet as you will be happy at discovering him.

The advantage of working with the breed rescue club is that they usually have good resources to defend the best interests of the dog. For instance, the dog may have been placed in a foster home or in kennels specializing in that breed. You may be lucky and be able to see the original home, the ideal situation because you can then get an idea of the habits of that household and of the dog's true character.

Almost all of the two-hundred-plus pedigree breeds of dogs have their own breed rescue clubs, whose offices may be contacted via either the American or the Canadian Kennel Clubs (see page 199 for addresses and phone numbers). Most of these voluntary societies do an excellent job and you can expect their staff to be as interested and critical about you as you might be about their breed or the dog you are considering.

## THE INHERITED DOG

There is an old saying, "What are families for if not for exploitation?" When it comes to animals in need of a home, that must be true. A pet may have been left to you in a formal and planned manner, perhaps in the will of a deceased relative. Alternatively, parents often get lumbered with their children's pets when that overseas assignment comes up, or cousin Jack moves from country house to city apartment where there is no space for a big dog. You may have reservations about the wisdom of taking on their pet, you may feel emotionally blackmailed, and forced into an unwise decision. If you have those feelings, just say no. Their pet is after all their responsibility and maybe you never did like it, or he just wouldn't fit in with the animals you already have.

On the other hand, the traditional extended family would automatically have offered hospitality and care to both the humans and the animals of relatives. It was a good system of care and share alike, just like canine society. It is for you to negotiate away any hard-to-take strings which might be attached, like feeding fish on Fridays, Sunday roast and daily trips to the seaside. When you take over there can be no obligation to return him to his original owners at some time in the future. To avoid any such misunderstanding within the family, it is better to have a formal deed of transfer. Perhaps a nominal sum of money should change hands and a receipt be given to confirm that the transaction took place.

## THE RETIRED SHOW DOG

Many among the professional show fraternity keep dogs they hope to win with or later to breed from. But maybe they are less successful than they had hoped, or they have a female dog which has been bred from many times but may no longer be useful to the breeder. You or I would naturally assume that such a person would love their dog so much that they couldn't bear to part with it and prefer to keep it as a pet. Not so for some (but not most) breeders: for them dogs are as much business as pleasure.

One thing is for certain in this mercenary world of dogs—don't pay big money to the breeder who offers you an adult, former show or breeding dog. You are doing them a favor by offering it a home and should not be subsidizing the breeder's business.

## THE VETERINARIAN

Vets and their staff are constantly being asked to euthanase animals that they do not wish to kill. Then too, there is the hard-luck case or the apparently unowned road-traffic-accident victim whom they treated as an emergency but no one appeared to collect the patient and pay the bill. Most veterinary surgeons would be delighted to hear that you are a prospective adopter of such an animal, or they will put you in touch with the local animal rehoming agencies.

## ADVERTISING

Scan any local newspaper and there is always the advertisement, "Free to a good home: beautiful Afghan, good with children, no vices, tel. . . ." Again, beware of dogs with a price tag. If it is a private advertiser, at least you will have the benefit of learning about the animal, his diet, training, and so on. But beware of the unscrupulous dealer in stolen dogs who sees the pet market as just an alternative to sale for animal experimentation.

## GLEANING A HISTORY

The adopted dog with a history will make a much smoother transition into your life and home than the completely unknown. If you do meet the original owner, or can contact them by telephone or letter, do so. Here is a checklist of questions you should try to have answered. They are not in any particular priority order, and I am sure you will think of additional questions tailored to your particular circumstances.

How old is X?

How old was he when you got him?

Where did you buy/acquire him?

Since puppyhood, is yours the only home he has had?

Do you have the address/phone number of the breeder?

Who is in your family (adults, children, ages, etc.)?

What sort of house do you live in?

Is there a garden?

Is there a park, woods or similar nearby?

Who walks X?

Is he let off the leash?

Does he pull?

Any other bad habits?

What do you feed X?

How many meals per day?

At what times is he fed?

Is he a fast or finicky eater?

Can you pick up X's feedbowl as he is eating?

Where does he sleep?

Can you (prospective adoptive owner) keep his bed?

Does he sleep on your bed?

Are there parts of the house from which he is excluded?

Do you keep other pets or animals?

How does X get along with them?

How would you describe X's general obedience?

Have you done any specific training?

Where, when, how, etc?

Is X regularly left alone?

If so at what time?

What's the longest he has ever been left on his own?

Does he damage things when left alone?

What is X's reaction to a knock at the door?

Has he ever bitten anybody?

Who?

Anyone else?

In total how many times has he bitten?

How do you punish X?

What else is he afraid of?

How about his reaction to thunder, loud bangs, etc?

How does he get along with strange dogs?

When is X at his happiest?

Doing what?

Who is his favorite person?

Why are you looking for another home for X?

Will you miss him when he's gone?

Has X been a healthy dog?

Who is X's usual vet?

When did you last go to the vet?

Any regular medication?

When was he last vaccinated?

Do you have his vaccination certificate (ask for it)?

Has X ever been in trouble with the law? For instance, has he strayed from home or produced a complaint about barking?

Has X ever had a major trauma or unpleasant thing happen to him? For instance, has he been attacked by another dog, or hit by a car?

The purpose of these questions is to provide a framework of knowledge to help you integrate the dog into your home and avoid the too-common presumptions of neglect, abuse or suffering in his previous life.

## WELCOME HOME, NEW DOG

When collecting your adopted dog, bring as many of his possessions as seems reasonable. At the very least, his collar, leash, feeding bowl, bed, toys, and any of those special things that a dog might accumulate. You may soon want or have to buy a new collar and a longer leash, but for the first few days normality should be the objective. Start as you intend to continue by having him sleep where he is to sleep long-term. Just because his previous owners had him sleeping in the bedroom there is no reason why you should do the same. If there were strict and regular mealtimes in his previous home, try to stick to them initially before gradually evolving your own timetable.

As for walking, it is best to keep the dog on a leash until you know a little more about him and until he has formed a bond with you and your surroundings. This may be the time to invest in an extending leash. Watch his reactions with other dogs carefully, as well as with traffic, joggers and all the other hazards of life. Be prepared for surprises.

As for discipline, the answer is don't! Your new companion is probably still confused by a change of environment and companions. Even bad owners are loved and missed by dogs; there will be a sense of loss or mourning for the old family. Taking a dog from kennels or a temporary foster home will reduce this grief reaction and anything is better than a life in kennels. But kennels may also have given him vices for you to work on. For instance, lack of opportunity to excrete outside the kennels can leave a residual house-training problem. Allow time, be tolerant, and dip into the pages of Part Three of this book for remedies if the problem is not self-resolving.

By adopting an adult dog rather than purchasing a puppy, you have made a personal statement against overproduction of puppies, and you probably saved a life from a prematurely sticky end. But setting emotion aside, the main beneficiary must be you and your family. A

Never say "no" when a rattle can works better. Shula used to steal food.

At the beginning of training, she runs to the booty.

Missile alert! Blame the booty, not the silent owner, for this unpleasant surprise.

Mimicry: Old dogs teach young dogs new tricks
better than master. Sam, Pollo and redundant owner.

My hero! Pollo apes Sam.

Start young and dental care becomes a daily pleasure.

Headcollars give kind control and simplify training:
Nutty *(right)* is wearing a Promise collar, Sam *(left)* a Halti.

Heel-work with a one-yard leash. No need for violent jerking just instrumental reward for walking alongside *(see pages 59-62)*.

"Heel" signaled by the click of an extending leash—left hand only, liberate the right *(see pages 59-62)*.

*Come!* Pollo to Emily Mugford.

*Down,* instrumentally taught.

# Teaching *fetch:*

First, agitate a favorite toy.

Throw it and call "fetch!"

Call "come" as he naturally returns it to you, his playmate *(see pages 65-66)*.

*Down* by following a tidbit to the ground
*(see pages 63-64).*

*Down* to a right-hand signal
*(see pages 63-64).*

*Sit* to a left-hand signal.

mere dog will soon become one of the family and adapt to your ways. You have saved on the usual puppy-penalties of chewed furniture and piddled-upon carpets; you have been able to leave this adult dog alone for half a day while you are at work, whereas a puppy needs constant supervision. All in all, the rehomed dog can be a best buy.

9

# A Dog's Dinner:
## Feeding for Good Behavior

A few years ago, I spent a happy afternoon stalking feral dogs in downtown St. Louis, Missouri. My particular quarry was a scruffy little half-bred beagle, and her three shaggy-coated pups, whose age I would guess at eight to nine weeks. They lived in a derelict part of town awaiting demolition and redevelopment, where they shared a basement with a few enterprising rats, cockroaches and the like. My interest in these dogs was to answer the straightforward question: How did they survive? Where was the food, the fresh water, and how did mom and pups spend their time? The answer was that mom made early-morning and late-evening forays into the surrounding, populated neighborhoods, where she stole, begged and rummaged through garbage.

All three strategies worked. I myself witnessed her skedaddling out of a house holding what looked like uncooked burgers and pursued by the resident dog of an irate householder. She raced back to her basement so fast that I was unable to keep up with her; she careered under fences and along routes blocked to this rather oversized canine ethologist. Then again, I saw her tearing open plastic trash bags for the chicken bones and other rich pickings left over from the table, and she also hunted, judging by the piles of feathers and one solitary rat tail,

*98*

which had become a toy for the pups. I managed to examine one of the puppies, and against all the odds it was well grown and could have done justice to any dog food commercial.

My encounter with this Missouri dog and her offspring raised two possibilities. Either American garbage makes extraordinarily good-quality dog food, or feral mutts are great survivors whose meals don't need to provide nutritional perfection. I suspect that both are true.

Yet most American dogs lead the lives of proverbial couch potatoes, popping in and out of their warm or air-conditioned houses to the yard for a woof at the mailman, and that's about it for the day. Where is the need for "nutritional perfection" in such a lifestyle?

Before I began my present career of behavior modification of problem pets, I spent nine happy years at a large pet-food company, researching the ins and outs of nutrition as it affects dog and cat behavior. Facilities available to me were the biological equivalent of Rolls Royce engineering labs; my colleagues had Ph.D.s in biochemistry, nutrition, digestive physiology, and there were clinicians, hematologists along with common-sense kennel staff. We were a tiny cog in a multimillion-dollar enterprise that filled tens of millions of cans with dog food for the world's hungry Fidos and pampered Rovers.

What are the scientific criteria for a good diet that guide researchers in the pet-food industry? Look at the list below:

- Palatability: that dogs will eat it
- Affordability: that owners will buy it
- Appearance: that owners think it looks right both for them and their pet
- Color: ideally meaty red-brown
- Profit: low-cost ingredients
- Firm stools: people do look at their pets' poops!
- Maintenance: that dogs can live on it
- Gestation and growth: complete nutrition for life

Notice that what you, sensible reader, might regard as the first priority—complete and reliable nutrition for life—comes last in the list; cosmetics and profit come well before. As they say, that's the free market, so the consumer must tread warily along the aisles of supermarkets crammed with crunchy this, chunky that and muesli for mutts. How can you possibly choose between these powerfully advertised brands with their conflicting claims about enjoyment, value, nutrition and the like? How do you feed a dog, let alone a puppy, and can you rely on the persuasive exhortations of the pet-food manufacturers? Would owners be better concocting their pets' meals at home like mother and certainly like grandmother used to do?

I am in no doubt that good value for money can be found in prepared pet foods; indeed that's what I feed my own trio of Sam, Nutty and Pollo. But each is fed differently, because one is a finicky eater (Sam) and has a hard-driving lifestyle dealing with my canine patients. Nutty is the total opposite of Sam, the proverbial Jack Spratt's fat wife because she hates unnecessary exercise, eats every fallen crumb, thrives on what she steals from our twin four-year-olds and if they are not around can always eat horse feed, even horse droppings! Of course, Pollo is a growing puppy, and we take special care about what he eats. Before suggesting some practical and specific criteria for feeding dogs, I should first present the general rules of feeding behavior and good nutrition. There are many, but I will just pick out the most important and sometimes neglected truisms here.

### Rule 1: feed frequently

When given the chance, dogs will take frequent, small meals: they are proverbial nibblers. What a contrast with the traditional view of their being gorgers, which sprang from the observation that a half-starved wolf can consume a gigantic meal if it is lucky in hunting (David Mech, the wolf biologist, observed one animal eat 40 percent of its own body weight from a kill in winter). But not many pet dogs are starving, and it turns out that they are more efficient calorie counters if they can eat a little, digest, absorb, then eat a little more. It's a drip-feed system as opposed to the occasional great flood. In my research, we found some dogs would take as many as twelve meals a day, others five, the average eight. A free-access, self-feeding regime only works if the foods offered to the dog are shelf-stable so that they don't become flyblown, infected or dried out. In practice, that means one of the many varieties of complete dry foods, as opposed to wet foods.

If Nutty, my fat corgi, were offered a mountain of food, she would become disgustingly overweight. But she would then demonstrate what physiologists call positive overshoot, where after her body weight had increased, compensatory mechanisms would cut back her intake to more normal levels. By contrast, the two setters in my life, and about one half of all pet dogs, would find the right balance of food intake and match it to energy expenditure. Practically, what does all this mean? For some dogs, an ideal regime would be one where the dog is given the opportunity to pick and choose when he or she fancies a munch. Let his own body determine when he eats and how much he eats rather than you, the owner.

For other dogs, there has to be strict regulation of energy intake, so a structured meal-feeding pattern set by the owner is required. However, that does not mean just one gorge-meal per day; better two, three, or, if you have the stamina (I do not), more. Whatever sort of dog you have, fat or thin, glutton or gourmet, the rule should be little and often.

### Rule 2: variety, the spice of life

In my pet-food researching days, it was my job to devise ways to measure enjoyment of food by dogs. It may sound bizarre, but I seriously did videotape dogs wagging their tails, measure the pauses between gulps, the size of each gulp of food, the time spent chewing before swallowing and so on. Then there are food preferences: did he eat Brand X in preference to Brand Y? By these and other criteria, the really important factor which showed up in my research was that dogs want variety: they look for new sensations. However, there are some interesting exceptions to this rule. The more timid or nervous the dog, the less likely it is to try out something new. That is because the more fearful and cautious an animal, the closer it is to adopting the wild dog strategy, where it must cautiously sample the food available to avoid eating potential poisons. When we domesticated the dog, we removed that cautiousness, which is why pet dogs are so vulnerable to consuming the chemical horrors to be found in homes and gardens today.

In practical terms, this means that it is sensible to change the type or at least the flavor of dog food from meal to meal. If you have a particularly finicky dog, the hors d'oeuvres concept can apply: offer a first course of food X, followed by second, even third courses of Y and Z. Make it all more like an eating-out experience at a good French restaurant, compared with the "throw-everything-together-on-a-plate" approach.

## Rule 3: the dietary culture—puppy experiences condition adult preference

Puppies that have been exposed to a variety of foods are less fussy in their food habits than those that are maintained upon only a restricted range of foods. This is particularly a phenomenon of the first twelve weeks of life, before the natural neophobia or conservatism of adolescence takes over. The practical moral here is that one should give puppies a changing menu of diets in the first few months of life, thereby providing the opportunity for a more varied and pragmatic approach to feeding later on. There are physiological benefits too, because offering a variety of foods helps puppy to establish a balanced gut flora, better able to ward off infection that may strike later on in life.

## Rule 4: water, the staff of life

The most important factor that we found, which determined how much dogs enjoy their food, is how wet it is. The more water, the faster they gulp the food, the more they prefer it and so on. Now water comes quite cheap, and there's no need to buy it in dog food cans when it pours fairly economically from the tap.

It is difficult to tell how much water there is in a dog food from just examining the packaging. You have to be a mathematician to overcome the cunning marketeers who will tell you the percentage of protein, fat, carbohydrate and ash but won't declare the largest single ingredient: water. For most canned foods, water levels can be as low as 75 percent, but more typically they are in the 80 to 84 percent range, i.e., only 16 percent may be useful food. Dry foods have to be below 10 percent moisture to be shelf-stable, and most contain 7 to 9 percent moisture. Finally, there are some hybrid products, not so popular nowadays, called semi-moist foods, which contain salts, sugar and chemicals to suppress fungal and bacterial activity. They have an intermediate moisture content of 25 to 30 percent.

Of course meat, and your dog's body, is also mostly water. In fact it is about 70 percent water, so why, you might ask, does the pet-food industry add yet more to the can when formulating dog food? They really do not need to, as can be gauged from the traditional canned corned beef product of South America which has a moisture content of only 55 percent, i.e., 45 percent is useful food. So a typical can of commercial dog food contains only one third of the useful nutrients (expressed on a dry weight basis) compared with corned beef, yet you would not guess that when examining a slice of dog food alongside a slice of corned beef. The reason one cannot guess the moisture content of canned pet foods or most other canned products is that the pet food industry uses large quantities of gelling agents: natural compounds from seaweed, beans and other sources that bind water and give it a stiffness, just like gelatine. In other words, the consumer loses two ways with canned dog foods: you get only a third of the food you think you're getting, and you actually pay for the clever technology that goes into binding surplus water to give it the wholesome appearance of what is actually completely useless glistening jelly or gravy.

## Rule 5: fiber—eat your vegetables

Wolves, and by association dogs, may be called carnivores, but they have to eat more than meat alone. In nature, I have seen wolves in the U.S. eating persimmon fruit, and wildlife studies indicate that, depending upon seasonal availability, grasses, roots and fruit can form a significant part of the wolf's diet. It's just the same with our dogs; some will kill for an apple core, others for a carrot, some even for cabbage—our corgi picks her own blackberries! There are several reasons why dogs might eat vegetables, but one explanation is that they need fiber in their diet. We know from the work of the late Dr. Denis Burkitt, a famous physician from Bristol, England, that people also need fiber. Interestingly, the dog's gut is similar to that of humans: we evolved for a hunter–gatherer's diet on the plains, where high-fat, high-protein foods are best balanced with vegetable fiber to "keep things moving" or, as the physiologists say, to reduce "transit time." Fiber comes in many forms and qualities. It all depends upon the length of the polysaccharide chains, assuming that the fiber source is a carbohydrate such as from cereals. However, animal materials also provide fiber, for instance from cartilage or connective tissue, but they are not as effective as vegetable fibers because the digestive enzymes of the gut are able to dissolve them.

We often see declared on foodstuffs its fiber content. You can assume that this is the useful fiber fraction, the bits that will not be dissolved by our or our dogs' digestive enzymes and that will pass through the body relatively unchanged. Cereals are the most useful source of crude fiber, be it from bran, the husk of cereals, even from chemically processed straw. Other good fiber sources are root vegetables, including the ubiquitous carrot. Commercially, fiber is produced in vast quantities from beets as a by-product of the sugar industry.

But surely high fiber means voluminous stools, and who needs to pick up elephantine feces behind one's pet? Certainly, it can be shown experimentally that a dog on a particularly low-fiber diet will end up defecating once every two to three days, but the residual material is the more revolting! That's because the indigestible residue has been sitting in the colon, at the end of the gut, for that same two to three days, nastily fermenting with unpleasant gas- and toxin-producing bacteria. By comparison, food will pass through the healthy dog's system in half a day, so there's less time for pathogenic bacteria to take hold before the fiber whisks them away. That's why the feces of dogs on high-fiber diets are so much less smelly than those on concentrated foods. Even worms can tell the difference. High-fiber feces are more rapidly eaten up and taken back into the soil than sticky, gelatinous, high-nitrogen, low-fiber feces from a dog kept on a low-residue diet.

In practical terms, this gives a major plus to most dry dog foods; but check, because just a few brands of these are also low in fiber. The majority, however, contain more than 5 percent, which is a good level. Of course it is easy to supplement fiber by giving your dog the occasional carrot, bran or even adding paper tissues to his rations. The behavioral bonus of high-fiber diets is that both you and your dog will have less of an urge to overeat; we won't so often experience that "I could eat a horse" hunger tension.

### Rule 6: dine together—social facilitation

In nature, where hunting is a collective enterprise, meals are something for the pack to have together. So it was not surprising for my research to reveal that domestic dogs living in groups tended to synchronize their trips to the trough. Furthermore, the size of meals or their appetite was greater when they ate together compared to when they ate alone.

Another interesting finding of our observations of groups of dogs eating together was that they *never* fought over food. Admittedly, the supply was generous and they had lived together since puppy days. Food-guarding and competitive feeding is only created in situations of uncertainty over the food supply. That need never arise in most pet situations; the dog can feel secure that the food put down is his to eat until he chooses to stop. In my professional role, I have always recommended owners not to take food away from their pet then return it, contrary to the advice often found in popular dog books. Certainly there should be no slapping on the nose if the dog growls.

I would rather we developed a more natural approach to feeding our dogs where their mealtimes coincide with ours, and that it became a social not a competitive event. I would certainly disregard the stern advice from one dog trainer turned "behaviorist" that you should achieve dominance and authority over your dog by making him wait for his food until you have had yours. That is not the way to get the dog on your side.

Finally, to obviate the need for competitiveness over food, it is a good idea to provide a ration in your puppy's or adult dog's bowl slightly less than he is likely to eat or need. When he nears the bottom of the bowl, add supplementary food, so you are seen to be the provider of manna, a welcome participant in the process of feeding. In other words, give rather than take away food from the dog.

### Rule 7: protein—taste or nutrition?

High-protein diets were all the rage among pet food companies and some nutritionists in the 1970s. More sober considerations of hunger among the world's people as well as results of clinical research into the causes of kidney and liver disease have changed that view. Now, more nutritionists would say that enough protein is enough, that the dog is as efficient at conserving and sparing protein as is man, and that it is wasteful to offer protein simply to be used as an energy source. Better the more economical energy sources of carbohydrate and fat.

As well as the total quantity of protein, the quality matters. Protein quality depends upon balanced profiles of amino acids, the building blocks from which proteins are formed. If food is denatured by extremes of heat, pH or microbial action during extended storage, its biological value or protein quality is reduced. Specifically, amino acids at the ends of protein chains drop off, or the chain itself is chemically fractured.

There has been considerable research into the quality of various proteins, those from fresh meat usually being high, but the same protein exposed to intensive heat processing (such as during the canning process) can be dramatically lower. It can drop from a typical 90-plus percent available protein from fresh meat to as low as 60 percent availability after extreme heat processing. Then again, the source of proteins affects their biological value. Connective tissue, skin and organs such as lungs have a lower biological value than good-quality muscle meats. These differences are never apparent from just examining the declared percentage protein content on the packet of dog food. Typically, canned foods provide 7 to 9 percent protein; in dry foods it is usually in the range 18 to 40 percent. The different moisture levels make the declared protein content meaningless, and since the quality of protein in pet food is almost never declared the consumer just can't compare brands. At a ludicrous extreme, shoe leather is high in protein but it provides poor nutrition for dogs!

As consumers, we have to place so much trust in the food manufacturers, hoping that they do after all select fresh ingredients that are not overprocessed or damaged in storage. Present-day labeling laws do not make these subtle distinctions, but veterinarians and experienced dog breeders get to know the diets that do and do not perform satisfactorily. What we desperately need is a clearinghouse for objective nutritional information about the various pet foods available on the market.

If high protein is not necessarily good, why is meat so much touted as the major ingredient of, say, canned dog foods? The reasons are in part the simple practical economics about availability of offal, blood and other by-products from the animal slaughter industry, which if they were not turned into pet foods, sausages and brawn, would be thrown away or turned into lower-value products such as fertilizer or farm animal feeds. Then again there is the question of palatability: there is no doubting that dogs like meat, and the chemistry of that liking has been explored by scientists in the pet-food industry. It turns out that all depends upon something called the Maillard reaction, where free amino acids chemically react with sugars. These produce the aroma of, for instance, roast meat and other savory flavors that are highly attractive to dogs. Nowadays, they can even be produced synthetically, as appetizing to dogs as the real thing from your oven at home. Many commercial dog and cat foods contain such synthetically derived flavors, though really they have no serious function except to encourage animals to overeat or apparently enjoy their food more in the eyes of doting owners like you and me.

Too much protein is bad for dogs, especially in their later years when kidney function might be impaired. At the Animal Behaviour Centre we have amassed evidence that high-protein dog foods can, in some dogs, induce massive changes in behavior shortly after a meal. Boarding kennels that have switched from a low-protein to a high-protein dry dog food have also reported bizarre changes in the behavior of their long-term inmates. One manager of a rescue center told me that most of his collies and collie crosses were "off the wall" when he switched to a widely advertised brand of high-protein, low-fiber dry dog food.

To summarize, dogs are omnivores, they like variety, they like little and often, and they like to eat with us. Most are easy to feed and thrive on most things placed before them. However, I wouldn't put all my trust in any one brand of dog food, but would rather suggest that two, even three brands be fed at successive meals.

The science of clinical nutrition for dogs with particular medical problems has developed enormously in the last few years. Veterinarians now have access to diets specifically designed for the diabetic patient, for fat dogs, dogs with ailing kidneys, skin and other allergies (a major and increasing problem), for finicky pets and convalescing dogs. The companies providing these diets can back up their claims with detailed research evidence, to a much greater extent than manufacturers of regular dog food from the supermarket. So if you want specific advice about feeding your pet, look to your veterinarian in this as in other matters.

## SPECIFIC FEEDING PROBLEMS

Many dogs carry the pear-shaped waistlines of their masters, others have the Twiggy look, and just a few dogs can become quite disturbed if they eat too much of the wrong foods. The parallel with the latest findings about human nutrition and psychiatry is quite remarkable, and I will deal with these three practical problems in the remainder of this chapter.

### The greedy eater

Obesity is a killer disease for dogs: it can precipitate the onset of diabetes, place strain upon the muscular-skeletal system, cause respiratory distress in hot weather that might lead to heart failure, and more. Contrary to popular belief, fat dogs are generally unhappy dogs, so if your pet has oozing ripples of waistline flab, consult your vet about slimming targets and a reduction program.

Not many owners have scales that are accurate or large enough to weigh dogs, but the well-equipped veterinary surgeon should have the scales for the job. Another method of weighing dogs is with bathroom scales. Weigh yourself, then pick up the dog and weigh yourselves together and subtract the first from the second. For the sake of calculating food intake, it is simplest to work with body weights in kilograms, food intakes in grams. To convert pounds and ounces to kilos or grams, remember there are 2.2 lbs. in a kg and one ounce equals 28 grams.

Suppose your dog weighs 15 kg but he would be better weighing 10 kg. The poor creature has somehow to lose 5 kg of flab. This can be done using a proprietary slimming diet from your vet, or simply by cutting down his usual rations. As a simple guide, feed two-thirds of the daily maintenance energy requirement for his target body weight, i.e., as though he were a 10-kg dog. The daily maintenance energy requirement (or MER) can be calculated from the formula $60 \times$ Wtkg $+ 40$, which compensates for variations in the ratios between body weight and surface area of dogs of different sizes. Dogs have an MER that ranges from 50 kcal/kg/day to 100 kcal/kg/day, the latter, higher figure being for small and more active dogs, while the lower figure is for the typically lethargic domestic dog of a large breed.

Our 15-kg dog (which should weigh 10 kg) has a daily maintenance energy requirement of 74 kcal/kg, and his daily food intake should therefore be 740 kcal. But we have decided to slim him down by feeding two-thirds of that level, i.e., only 500 kcal/day.

Of course, we don't offer food in the form of calories, we offer it as weights or volumes. You must now understand that foods vary greatly in their energy density, from 350 kcal/100 g for many dry and soft moist foods, to as low as 75 kcal/100 g for "premium" canned foods. Let us suppose that the canned food you are giving a fat dog has an energy density of 100 kcal/100 g. Then our candidate for slimming should be given:

$$\frac{740 \times 0.66 \times 100}{100} = 488 \text{ g canned food}$$

Alternatively, if we are supplying him only with a complete dry food, his daily requirements would be as follows:

$$\frac{740 \times 0.66 \times 100}{350} = 140 \text{ g}$$

Weigh the dog each week and aim for a loss in body weight of about 1 percent, maximum 2 percent per week. In our example we are aiming for a slow weekly body weight loss of 100 to 200 g per week, from a starting point of 15 kg to the target weight of 10 kg. As he reaches his target, gradually return rations to 100 percent of his calculated daily maintenance regime.

Throughout this slimming period, the dog will be hungrier than usual, more motivated to steal, beg and manipulate humans into breaking the slimming program. You can ease this process by the following tips:

*Increase exercise,* so there are a lot of interesting outdoor activities before meals and distractions to interrupt food-soliciting behaviors.

*Multiple meals* are better than a large meal once a day.

*Fiber* provides the slimming dog with something for his guts to work on.

*Prandial chewing.* When wild dogs eat they have to tear flesh off the bone, often consuming the bone itself. This means they have to expend considerable masticatory effort at mealtimes. The fine-textured pap of so many modern, prepared pet foods does not give the same dental work-experience as whole carcasses, so it is a good idea to redirect his chewing onto soft but non-nutritive items such as rubber toys. There is always a healthy debate among veterinary surgeons about the wisdom of bones, because so many dogs suffer obstructions and dental problems as a result of chewing hard bones. If your dog is sensible and patiently gnaws at bones rather than trying to crack them, offer large beef knuckle bones, which are better raw than cooked. Cooking hardens bones and makes them more likely to fracture dogs' teeth. Toys made of natural rubber are treated by dogs as food items; they are soft and a better outlet for chewing than natural bones. Alternatively, rawhide chews probably have a useful abrasive effect upon the surface of the dog's teeth, helping to remove food particles and plaque.

*Ambush theft?* The popular dog-training literature is replete with various methods of punishing dogs that steal food: ruses like a baited mousetrap, rattling tin cans which crash down on the dog when it steals the Sunday dinner, electric shocks applied to the door of a refrigerator that the dog has learned to raid, and so on. I am certain that the writers who have suggested such techniques have not proved them in practice, and my experience is that they are unnecessary, potentially dangerous and usually ineffectual.

Another technique that is often suggested to discourage a dog from stealing a particular food (e.g., sausages) is to taint them with hot pepper sauce or mustard. This assumes that the dog has a rather low level of intelligence and a poor ability to discriminate between mustard-tainted and untreated sausage. In my experience, this approach is always flawed—it is better to attend to the underlying causes of a dog's greed rather than to the particular outlet or symptom. It is more important to hide away food, fit reliable fastenings to cupboards and refrigerators, and clear work surfaces.

*Home dental care.* Finally, after meals of any description and for any dog, clean their teeth in the manner described on page 129.

It goes without saying that tidbits are out for training a dog that is excessively food-orientated. His drooling in anticipation of the possibility of food is both physiologically and psychologically unkind, maybe even unkind for carpets and clothes on which the slobbering dog rubs his chin.

### The finicky eater

I estimate that about 10 percent of pet dogs are finicky or difficult eaters; they will only eat palatable and refined foodstuffs or in extreme cases will even demand to be fed by hand. This might be unhealthy for the dog, it is hard on the family budget and tiresome having to fend off accusations from well-meaning dog lovers that you are starving your dog. I speak with immense experience of this problem, having owned two Irish setters which, in their early and more crazy years, both looked like russet-colored bags of bones rather than the pride and joy of an animal expert! I have had ample opportunity to determine the behavioral and other factors which stimulated or depressed appetite in dogs like Sam and his predecessor Bip, and this is what they taught me:

*Warm food.* Bringing food to body temperature significantly increases its palatability, more like a fresh kill than cold carrion to a wolf.

*Underfeed.* It may seem a paradox, but try never to feed the finicky dog more than it will eat; instead offer less than you think, from prior experience, he will readily consume. You will then keep a slight edge on his appetite, an uncertainty about whether the food might "run out." As the program develops, slightly increase the volume offered. Certainly do not offer a gigantic plate of food that he can pick over in several snacks through the day.

*Gorge feed.* This is opposite advice to that given for the greedy eater: feed one or, at most, two meals each day rather than several small meals. This will enhance the tendency toward competitive feeding (see below).

*Competition peps appetite.* If you have a cat that is on good terms with your dog, feed them side by side, even from the same bowl. Cats are marvelous manipulators and stimulators of canine competitive instincts. My dear-departed setter Bip would go into a decline of near-starvation when our tabby cat Boots was not about to share his food bowl. What you should not do is allow yourself to be used as a facilitator or competitor. If you do, his feeding will become contingent upon your presence and you will become a slave, his nursemaid. Never hand-feed unless the dog is seemingly on the verge of clinical starvation, in which case also seek urgent veterinary advice.

*Concentrated foods.* The body's energy-regulating mechanism can easily be tricked by offering foods that are high in fats and thus of a high energy density. Whatever the diet you have selected to give your dog, it can be enhanced in energy density by the addition of animal or vegetable fats such as drippings from roast meat or sunflower oil. In addition, feed diets which are low in fiber.

*The dinner party.* Feeding time should be party time for the dog, and his meals should coincide with yours. If it helps, feed the finicky dog beside the dining table.

So much about the beauty of dogs is in the mind of the beholder, and what to one person looks like a starveling whippet is to another sleek perfection. Breeds vary enormously in the "set point" of the body's ponderostat, the mechanism that instructs the appetite to eat or to fast. You and I may judge that my corgi Nutty is fat, but her ponderostat disagrees! So it is with the skinny whippet or saluki. So do consider your dog's happiness before imposing either a strict slimming or fattening regime on your would-be body-beautiful pet.

## Diet and dog behavior

In the medical literature, there are many examples of our psychological states being affected by what we eat. In some cases the effects can be quite extreme, as when hypersensitive individuals take coloring agents such as tartrazine (E102), which can rapidly provoke dramatic mood changes. I have always been fascinated by the possibility that the mood of a dog may also be affected by what it eats, and there is now an increasing body of clinical evidence to suggest that that is indeed the case. Some dogs are allergic to specific components of foods, be it a meat protein source, a gelling agent or a carbohydrate source (wheat gluten, for instance). The effects can be spectacular, causing diarrhea, skin problems, discomfort, depression or hyperexcitability.

During the early years of our practice, I discovered a clear association between what irritable and sometimes aggressive golden retrievers were fed and their behavior. If fed on high-protein, canned foods, they would be moody and alternately depressed and dangerously aggressive; whereas if they were placed on a simple, home-prepared and moderate-protein diet, the symptoms disappeared. After that early finding on golden retrievers, we have seen many more instant "miracle" changes in dog behavior as a result of changing their diet. It is a complicated subject with many factors involved, including the breed of dog, various gastro-enterological pathologies, early sensitization to particular foodstuffs and the like. At the Animal Behaviour Centre we recommend the following home-prepared low-protein recipe to check out a possible diet–behavior connection:

1. One part boiled white meat: chicken, mutton, fish or rabbit.
2. Four parts boiled white or brown rice, or mashed potato.
3. A commercially sold vitamin–mineral supplement.
4. Vegetable oil, e.g., sunflower oil—one tablespoon/10 kg or 22 lbs. body weight.

If there is an improvement in behavior on this 1:4 mixture, it can be used as the routine maintenance diet. Alternatively, a low-protein prescription diet in dry or canned forms may be obtained from veterinary surgeons.

# 10

# Equipment:

## The Good, the Bad and the Nasty

Man has been ingenious in devising equipment to control and train the horse, and every equine activity has characteristic designs of bridles, bits, saddles and the rest. Specialized items of harness are used by the horse fraternity for particular personalities, problems or styles of riding. For some reason, dogs have not attracted the same level of inventiveness as horses, and they are the worse off for it. But times are changing, and the last decade has seen some quite new concepts that have dramatically affected the care and welfare of animals. Specifically, design technology has much to contribute to the ancient practice of dog training.

### CANS

Landfill sites the world over are filling every day with an estimated billion cans produced for the food and soft-drinks industries. Only a few are recycled, so you can take a personal initiative in easing the garbage crisis by finding a new use for soft-drink containers: as rattle tin cans for dog training.

Take four pebbles, pop them in the can and seal over with tape.

Make up several, trying to select the same make of can and sizes and number of pebbles, so that they sound the same. If the can becomes distorted in use and develops sharp edges, recycle it and make up another.

The can will become a classically conditioned stimulus, an all-purpose interrupter and disincentive, a warning that danger lurks and a substitute for the word "No" from human lips. The concept of a thrown device in dog training is not a new one: even Konrad Most used chains to throw at dogs. Others have suggested throwing so-called training disks, Wellington boots, even bunches of keys, the intention being actually to hit the dog with the object on the first few occasions. For Colonel Most and the many trainers who have pla-giarized his approach, the throw chain was a convenient inducement to obey a command. My use of the rattle can is quite different, in that it aims to create a superstitious fear of the sound of a can by surprise rather than by physical contact. Gradually that fear is developed by repetition and surprise, but never allow Fido to discover that the can is, after all, just a tin can.

For both behavioral therapy and dog training, we have selected the can rather than a bunch of keys, a boot or a chain because cans are light, soft, rounded and free. If by some mischance your aim fails and the dog is hit by a can, it will not come to any harm, whereas chains, metal disks or sharp keys could blind him.

Training with a rattle can could begin at any age, but is most conveniently done with the young puppy, say at the age of twelve or thirteen weeks instead of saying No. The method of application is the same for puppies as for adults, except that the speed with which puppies form a stable and long-lasting classically conditioned re-sponse to the can is better than with adults. At the Animal Behaviour Centre, we estimate that one in five adult dogs fail to form a long-term response to the rattle can, whereas failure rate among puppies is fewer than one in twenty.

Your dog's first exposure to the rattle can is the most critical in determining its future strength as a negative reinforcer. Ideally, he will not have seen you carrying it, so avoid casually rattling it or allowing the dog to check it out: carry it secretly in your pocket or position it somewhere out of reach. At the moment the dog performs an unde-sired act such as jumping up, running far ahead in heel training, or stealing the cat's food, toss the can within a one-meter radius. Retrieve and remove it immediately: don't permit puppy or dog to play with it.

Repeat the exercise on two, or at most five further occasions, by which time a reliable and deepening conditioned fear should have been induced. Throughout, stay quiet, so that your voice does not become associated with this negative experience. For instance, do not shout the dog's name, and certainly not "No!" or "Leave!"

Comfort the dog if his fear seems profound and long-lasting, and for such dogs, do not throw the can again; be content with the mildest rattle. Use of the can depends on your judgment in assessing the fearfulness and vulnerability of your dog: Pavlov referred to inhibited versus excitable canine personalities in relation to their ease of conditioning. For example, a typical Labrador would be an inhibited type, a border collie an excitable one. It is much easier to induce a conditioned fear rapidly in a border collie than in the more phlegmatic Labrador.

Once you detect a reliable fear response in your dog of retreat and ears back, go easy on further use of the can. Remain highly selective in the situations where it is used, reserving it for the occasions when other forms of distraction or response substitution training are not effective. The can runs the risk of becoming a symbolic version of the dog trainer's biggest stick, an all-purpose devil that could induce a neurotic fear if used too crudely or too frequently. My experience is that it can become a liberating force for both dogs and their owners, because it does away with the need for harsh corrective methods and you can distance yourself from the can. Always work to the minimum level of stimulation sufficient to produce the desired response: multiple rattles will tend to produce extinction of the conditioned fear. The objective should always be for brief surprise followed by calm learning.

## COLLARS

There is a wonderful museum of dog collars at Leeds Castle, Kent, where one can see that man has adorned dogs with an array of them for 5,000 or more years. They vary from woven silk collars for pampered aristocratic pets to outward-facing metal spikes on the collars of war dogs. It is obvious that in nature, the wolf does not adorn itself with a collar, so bear in mind that they are always unnatural devices which interfere with body language and the touch sensations of the wearer. Nevertheless, the neck is a practical part of the body through which to make a link with a human, the modern world being too dangerous to have dogs running free. There are four types of collars.

## Flat collars

This traditional collar used to be manufactured only from leather, with a metal buckle and ring for the attachment of leash and identity tag. The design may be thousands of years old but it remains my favorite, and should not harm the dog. When selecting a flat collar, aim for one that spans two cervical vertebrae. As a guide, for a Labrador-proportioned dog this means an inch. For a toy poodle, half an inch would be right, whereas a Great Dane might do best with a collar as much as three inches wide. The most elegant of all collars are those traditionally worn by greyhounds and whippets, and they are probably the safest, with their wide coverage under the throat.

More modern and more reliable material than leather for the construction of dog collars is woven nylon or, cheaper and less attractive, polypropylene. These webbing collars are virtually everlasting, whereas a leather collar can scarcely be relied upon to last a year. I have suffered the extreme embarrassment and not inconsiderable danger of the worn leather of a dog's collar breaking at some critical moment of behavioral therapy, so I now usually substitute nylon for leather before walking my patients into danger.

## Choke chains

No dog deserves to be adorned with the strangulating links of the choke chain, and yet it is the most commonly used item of dog training equipment at exhibitions, shows and everywhere where dogs are walked. How did such a bizarre affront to the rights of dogs to a pain-free association with man come about? I have been unable to find out who first invented this instrument of torture, but it was probably a farmer with some chain that just happened to be lying around in his stables or cow sheds. By the end of the last century and in the era of Konrad Most, their use in Germany was widespread. They were then introduced to the U.S., the U.K. and elsewhere, as German dog-training methods spread after World War I. The choke chain became the essential instrument of compulsion and induction in the Most method, to be plagiarized and adapted by most writers on the subject since: from William Koehler in the U.S. to Barbara Woodhouse in the U.K., and even by some contemporary writers who misleadingly claim to be trendy and gentle.

My best guide to whether or not a trainer has an acceptable attitude toward dogs is whether or not he carries a choke chain in his pocket. If choke chains are insisted upon in a training class, make a point of debating the issue in front of trainers and other owners, and then walk out. Most dog training books illustrate how the choke should be correctly applied, so that it releases when the dog slackens. Unfortunately, my experience of rescuing animals from illegally placed snares, which are essentially choke chains made of wire, is that they can garotte just as effectively when worn the "right" as well as the "wrong" way.

One could tolerate choke chains if they provided some remarkable benefit to the dog in training, perhaps by speeding it up or making it simpler. That is not my experience: the purpose of a collar is first to restrain the dog from entering into danger, and secondly as a device to deliver a discreet signal or touch stimulus to the neck. The problem with the choke chain is that it produces a compound sensation for the dog. In quick succession there is the jangle of metal, constriction of tissues, pulling of hair by entrapment in the links of the chain and finally arresting of forward movement. A flat collar is much more efficient at delivering the discriminative stimulus of a light touch to the neck, which is all that is required.

Don't imagine that some choke chains are less cruel than others. Mrs. Woodhouse advocated her particular design of flat-ringed links, others prefer links so fine that they function like a cheese cutter, while yet others have heavy-duty links the size of farmers' traditional cow chains. Choice of one type over the other has no scientific basis, but can serve as a personality test of the trainer.

A more recent innovation has been to use fabric chokers, particularly encouraged by certain American trainers and also promoted in Britain. The manner of fitting as recommended by this transatlantic school of dog training is that the choker be worn particularly high around the dog's neck, just behind the ear. This happens to be one of the body's most sensitive acupuncture points, well-known to Chinese torturers and no place to be assaulting a dog.

I first exposed the dangers of choke chains in an essay published in 1980. My conclusion now, as then, is: if you care for your dog, chuck the choke!

## Pinch and spike collars

Man's underlying attitude to his animals just gets worse when we look at the damage that can be done by the spiked collars, too commonly employed in the U.S. and in continental Europe but, thankfully, rarely in the U.K. They unashamedly work by the application of pain, and one can only imagine the degree of local tissue damage that is inflicted by these devices. In the early 1980s, I was presented with a weimaraner as a patient at our Paris clinic; she was said to be uncontrollable and wore a spiked collar. Her naive owner had already complained that she had punctured her trachea while using the spiked collar. "This dog just will not learn," were her words.

My advice to those who encounter a trainer or a pet store marketing these devices is to protest at their cruelty; easily done in the U.K. but requiring more courage and conviction in other countries.

## The half-choke

The half-choke is an easily adjusted collar that closes snugly onto the dog's neck but should not actually choke it. Ideally, a flat surface of leather or nylon webbing contacts the underside of the dog's neck, so that the sliding chain mechanism does not become entangled in the dog's fur. The advantage of this design over the traditional flat collar is that the dog cannot slip or back out of his collar, and the better designs are adjustable as the dog grows. This is particularly useful for dogs with necks as wide as their heads. However, an undersized half-choke will choke just as surely as a real choke chain, so be sure that it is adjusted to the circumference of your dog's neck.

## EXTENDING LEASHES

One of the most useful inventions for the dog in the twentieth century was the extending leash concept. Its role in teaching dogs to walk and heel and in "come" training is described in Chapter 6, where I draw particular attention to the importance of the "clunk" sound effects that can be obtained by lightly depressing the brake button as one swings the leash out of its housing. That sound becomes an important discriminative stimulus for dogs.

The delight of the extending leash is that it provides a compromise between freedom and control. A light-handed approach to training virtually depends upon the use of an extending leash, at least in its early stages. Once the dog has learned to move his body in relation to the trainer in the relatively free fashion made possible by an extending leash, one can graduate to conventional leashes and later to no leash at all.

There is only one danger with an extending lead, and that is if you grab the free-running line to control the dog instead of using the push-button brake. If you do this, you will sustain a rope burn, which could be serious. I strongly recommend that you hold the extending leash in the left hand if it is intended that the dog walks on your left, in the right if it is to walk on the right. The free hand can hold tidbits, a tin can, this book or the hand of one's other best friend.

In inexperienced hands, the extending leash can get dog owners into a tangled state, and potentially place pets in danger. Remember that on any leash, the dog is free to move in the arc of a circle to either side, which from a pavement could mean stepping into traffic. Without intelligent monitoring of the dog's movements, the leash can likewise become entangled around the legs of people or other animals. The extending leash therefore requires constant and active participation by the owner-trainer; it is never a passive system of control.

A more recent development, of which I was co-inventor, is an extending leash incorporated into the dog's collar. The objective here is that the dog will always carry his own leash, which brings with it advantages of both convenience and simplified training. It means that you can never use the absence of a leash as an excuse not to walk the dog, nor have it out of control. Functionally, it reduces the contrast between running free and being on the leash with owner in control. There is no fiddly process of attaching leash to collar; you just reach for the handle. In competitive dog training and agility where there may be a frequent requirement for the dog to be on then off the leash, the leash in a collar is a delight.

## HANDS

It may seem strange to the reader that I have referred to the human hands as equipment, but so far as contact with your dog is concerned, that is what they are.

Traditionally, they have often been misused as instruments of pun-ishment for the strike behind the ear or the "tap" on the nose. As you will gather, I believe that that role of hands has expired, but there remain alternative and more important roles for hands in dog control.

Hands are important vehicles for reinforcement of desired behavior in dogs, both directly by tactile stimulation (i.e., massage) and indirectly by transporting goodies such as tidbits. From the moment of birth, most of our interactions with dogs are through hands, whereas in nature wolves or dogs interact with their heads and by licking around the mouth. We can turn our cupped hands into mock buccal cavities by spitting into them and letting our dogs lick them in affectionate reunion. Most dogs have a passionate desire to lick our faces, and it is so easy to redirect them to our hands. It is obvious that hands should be relied upon as instruments of instruction and kindness, without any possible association with punishment. Severe conflict leading to distressing behavioral pathologies can arise if hands give both pleasure and pain.


## HARNESSES

Harnesses spread the load from the point of attachment of a leash over the shoulders and beneath the belly of the dog. In the draft horse, such an arrangement is used to reduce local pressure from the collar, and in dogs, too, harnesses can stimulate pulling. However, the problem can be easily overcome by using the several approaches to teaching "heel" outlined in Chapter 6: the click of an extending leash, the rattle of a can, speeding up one's walking and reinforcing the proximity of the dog.

Harnesses are especially good on dogs that have short, thick necks, like pugs, notorious for their skill at slipping out of conventional collars. There are also orthopedic cases where any undue pressure or movement of the neck could cause pain and potential long-term damage.

Appreciation of the potential dangers of dogs in cars has led to the development of restraint harnesses for dogs. Once dogs have adapted to such restraint on the rear passenger seat of the car, they provide security for the dog in the event of an accident, making the frightened dog less likely to escape into the road and be killed. Road safety experts have many times pointed out the danger of having an unrestrained dog in the car; sudden braking can so easily turn the family pet into an airborne missile.

## HALTERS

The halter revolution may have been given a kick-start by myself in the 1980s, but really it goes much further back in time. An uncle of mine brought back from Belgium in World War I a photograph of draft dogs wearing halters, and even from the seventeenth century there are paintings of dogs wearing something that bears a passing resemblance to a halter. Nothing in this world is ever new!

There are two basic designs of halter. First, there is the patented Halti system with a nosepiece that acts independently of a collar piece and that slides through a ring under the chin. The second general category of halter is based upon a figure-eight design, where a single ring links two loops together. This concept has been developed and copied by many manufacturers and dog enthusiasts, so that now there are a number of different designs of halters. Unfortunately, they all suffer the disadvantage of requiring tight fitting to the dog, and the point of attachment is tucked under the animal's throat rather than forward and nearer to his nose. Accordingly, there is more of a tug action on the main core of the dog, rather than the light, head-moving steering action characteristic of the Halti.

The Halti has the added advantage of both permitting completely unrestrained mouth opening (i.e., panting to keep cool), and, if the dog is aggressive, barking or otherwise misbehaving, gently closing his mouth. This is simply done by lifting the lead, when the nosepiece tightens around the dog's jaws by sliding through the ring. This precise on-off mechanism of control over the dog's mouth makes the Halti an ideal instrument for behavior modification.

There is no minimum or maximum age at which halters might be fitted to a dog, but practically it is not usually necessary on puppies until they are sixteen weeks old. There are so many alternative ways of teaching basic control in puppies, as I have outlined in the twenty-week system. Of all adult dogs, I estimate that about 25 percent benefit from wearing a Halti; the remainder can be trained and controlled wearing a traditional wide collar.

Haltis used to be confused with muzzles, which they certainly are not. They have now achieved broader acceptance, and for instance are used by professional dog trainers from the guide dog and seeing eye organizations, assistance dogs for the disabled, the military and police. In our practice, we are constantly learning new applications of the halter approach, but the greatest single advantage is that it places the small, the frail and the uncertain in firm control of the dog, no matter what its size and strength. In Britain, where the law on dogs is much stricter than before, owners really do have to be in control, because the description "dangerously out of control" can now mean death to the dog.

## IDENTITY

It is a legal requirement that dogs wear some form of identification at all times; as a practical minimum, the name of the owner and home telephone. A number of identity schemes have been promoted— tattooing with various local and national registries, wearing a traditional tag on the collar and insertion of an electronic tag beneath the skin. All have their advantages and disadvantages, but an easily read and permanent name tag on metal or plastic is, in my view, indispensable. For the small sum and forethought that preparation of such a disk entails, a great deal of worry, risk and expense can be avoided should the dog get lost.

The disadvantage of tattooing is that it requires the services of a skilled operator, which can be expensive. Then again there is the problem of reading tattoos, which are usually numbers on the inside hind leg or in the ear of the dog. Some owners regard the latter as unsightly, and not all dogs are prepared to allow a stranger to peer under their hind leg. I know from experience the difficulty of deciphering the mucky blue spots of a badly performed tattoo.

The ID system of the nineties is undoubtedly the electronic chip, which is usually marketed and fitted by veterinarians. Many vets and most animal rescue and welfare agencies hold the readers, which recognize specially coded transmitters positioned just beneath the skin in the neck–shoulder area. Each chip emits a unique signal that can be matched to the owner's name and address from a central computerized registry. I have good reason to be grateful to the Identichip system, it having once retrieved my salacious setter, Sam, from our local RSPCA kennels, when he was enticed to roam in pursuit of a dog in heat. The disadvantage of these electronic tags is that there are at least four competing and incompatible systems on the market and the reader for one will not recognize a competitor's tag. The reader and encoder are not cheap so will not be available to all dog wardens or rescue agencies. Worst of all is the problem experienced with one design of electronic tag that tends to migrate away from the usual injection site behind the neck, so a dog may seem to be tag-negative when really he is positive!

## LEASHES

Dogs usually walk better off the leash than on because they dislike restriction. Accordingly, if we want a dog to walk in a more relaxed and precise relationship with us it is better to use a longer rather than a shorter leash. Aside from the extending leashes described earlier, leashes should be of greater rather than shorter length. A practical length is three to four feet, preferably with some degree of adjustability. Worst of all are short leashes, some no longer than a mere handle. The material of which leashes are made should be considered carefully, chain being uncomfortable to the hands, slippery in the cold and a source of distracting noise when rattled. Leather is always the most pliable and comfortable in all weathers, but unless maintained and oiled it will deteriorate. Wide nylon or cotton webbing is the practical leash for all weathers and it copes with the neglect that most of us heap upon our dog's equipment.

## MUZZLES

The obvious way to control a dog's potential for biting is to muzzle it. In some countries, dogs have to be muzzled at all times in public places. I believe that this restriction is excessive, but certainly there are times when many dogs are usefully muzzled, for instance, when being examined in a high-threat situation at the vet's, when being groomed or when receiving first aid. Muzzles are the most efficient means of stopping dogs from licking themselves after surgery, or self-mutilating, but they have an especially important role in the management of canine behavioral problems.

In our practice at the Animal Behaviour Centre, fully 60 percent of our canine patients are aggressive, and treatment that includes wearing a muzzle is recommended for about half of them. Sometimes, we muzzle only in the early stages of therapy, when we cannot be sure that treatment will be a success. It may be that the dog attacks other dogs or cats, bites children or is coprophagic, and that the risks of more such catastrophic incidents remain too high.

There are several factors that need to be considered in selecting the muzzle, the most important being the requirement of dogs to pant freely in order to stay cool. Some 90 percent of the dog's body heat is lost by the clever mechanism of resonant panting, where rapid but shallow vibrations of the diaphragm move a small volume of inspired air through the nose and across the nasal gland mucosa, to be expired through the mouth. Little physical energy is consumed by this clever mechanism, which is quite distinct from deep respiratory breathing, where the whole chest cage expands and contracts. The dog is one of several species that have come to rely for heat loss largely upon the nose, as opposed to the sweat glands with which we humans keep cool.

If muzzles must allow dogs to open their mouths, it is obvious that any design which restricts mouth opening is potentially dangerous. There are several that are sold commercially, manufactured from webbing or a fabric sleeve to clamp the jaws closed. Such muzzles are suitable only for brief restraint, such as at the vet's.

At times when the dog is given freedom to run and warm up in exercise, the box designs of muzzle are the best. They should allow the dog to pant freely, drink and even bark if they are to be humane. It is vital to select a size appropriate to the dog's nose and head proportions, for which owners should consult a veterinary surgeon or a knowledgeable person at a pet store. At the Animal Behaviour Centre, we usually use the Baskerville design, which is manufactured from lightweight and washable plastic, and can be easily fitted and removed. Dogs quickly get used to wearing their Baskerville muzzle, but it is essential that dogs wearing any muzzle be supervised, in case it becomes trapped or damaged.

## TECHNOLOGY TRAINERS

The inventiveness of human beings has been applied to some of the outstanding challenges of dog training, not least being how to deliver signals and punishment to dogs at a distance. In this section, we look at several commercially available devices, from the viewpoint of both animal welfare and effectiveness.

## Shock collars

The means to deliver a radio-controlled electrical shock to dogs has been around for forty to fifty years, and such devices are now commercially available in most countries. Historically, animal welfare societies and other responsible bodies have been opposed to the use of such devices in dog training, and that is also my view. The objections are both philosophical and practical. First, punishment becomes too easily available to the owner and can act as a substitute for intelligent training. Many of these devices are electrically unsafe, and are liable to deliver a painful shock to the animal when, for instance, there is radio interference from a passing aircraft, CB radio user or ham radio. Sometimes, the power of electrical shocks can be excessive and variable, especially when the equipment becomes wet. From an animal-learning standpoint, a shock collar can have disastrous consequences if the animal develops superstitious fears based upon the place and context in which it was punished. Formerly "safe" environments known to the dog suddenly become unsafe, as the animal is thrown into a high-risk detective puzzle to unravel the source and reason for punishment. There is only one application of shock collars that I can ethically justify: to train problem dogs that chase and kill livestock. Even here, there are several kinder alternatives that should be tried before the last resort of the shock collar.

One of the nastiest applications of shock collars is in a U.S.-manufactured invisible fence training system, where dogs are given a painful electrical shock when they stray across a buried wire. It allows people to have dogs loose in an open-plan garden without traditional fencing, but at a terrible cost to the dog's welfare. Instead of the dog being safe inside his own territory, passing strays can cross the invisible fence with impunity, attack the resident and, worse, chase him out of his garden, where he will be effectively marooned. The traditional security of home territory is replaced by an invisible fear of shock.

## Anti-bark collars

Electrical shock has also been incorporated into a device which is activated by a dog barking. It can be activated either by a microphone or a sensor which nestles under the dog's throat. Such anti-bark shock collars are widely used and abused, and vary in their electrical safety from those that deliver a single painful electrical shock after each bark, to others that incorporate delays, variation in intensity and programmable frequencies of shocks. My conclusion, which is largely based on the experiences of experts in other countries, is that they are disastrous devices that can induce extreme fear. They are often employed to stop dogs barking when left alone, which is, of course, one symptom of a separation anxiety (see page 165). It is always wrong to punish the dog for expressions of panic, especially in what should be the reliably safe environment of its own home.

An entirely different approach to the suppression of barking is offered by the Aboistop, which emits a stream of scented material (oil of citronella) when the dog barks. Extensive trials in France indicate that 90 percent of dogs wearing an Aboistop permanently stop barking when wearing the device, and in the U.K. a trial at the Animal Behaviour Centre showed that it can help solve a great variety of behavioral problems. Not only does the Aboistop stop barking, but it also stops the activity which might follow barking. For instance, Aboistop can help treat the territorial dog that barks before he bites a visitor, dogs aggressive toward other dogs, hysterical travelers in the car, and dogs with various compulsive disorders. The smell of citronella seems to disrupt normal sequences of behavior by evoking a spirit of investigation. The dogs never appear frightened, rather they go into sniff-and-search mode. The Aboistop should not be seen as a magical cure-all for any barking, rather as part of a considered and balanced approach to behavioral control.

### Noise generators

The characteristics of sound are defined by its frequency (from low-frequency infrasound to high-frequency ultrasound) and its intensity or volume. Sound is as important a medium for transmitting information in dogs as it is in other animals, but for training we can also use novel and loud sounds to attract investigation. There are two such devices available: the aerosol alarm, and ultrasonic emitters.

Aerosol alarms emit sounds in the very loud range 110–120 decibels, over a broad spectrum of frequencies. It was originally devised as an anti-mugging or rape alarm for humans, but has been modified to have a higher-frequency sound output than in the anti-human version. Trials at the Animal Behaviour Centre over many years show that nine out of ten dogs react initially to aerosol alarm, and some eight out of ten continue to react in the long term. Of course, a minority are either deaf or simply sound-insensitive! Applications of aerosol alarm are primarily to interrupt out-of-control and extreme-emergency situations, such as when two or more dogs are fighting or threatening to attack a person. By far the most sensitive types of dogs to those alarms are collies and their derivatives, the least sensitive being gundog breeds such as Labradors.

Electronically generated ultrasound has interested me since I began our animal behavioral practice. Most dogs are more sensitive than people to high-frequency noises. So, ultrasonic devices might be useful in training. Unfortunately, most of the commercially made devices emit a low intensity of sound, detectable over only a short distance. In tests at the Animal Behaviour Centre, we recorded a 30 percent consistent response to these ultrasonic emitters, and fewer than that were actually frightened of the ultrasound. We concluded that it is not ethical to market these ultrasonic devices as dog deterrents; they confer only a small measure of protection on someone liable to be attacked by dogs. On the other hand, for just a small minority of dogs they are useful as a training aid to signal some special event or circumstance.

The stage show *Annie* stars a small mongrel dog who has to perform several key actions under noisy circumstances. I was briefly involved as a consultant for the West End production, and we selected an ultrasonic signal as the cue for Sandy to engage in excited and antagonistic barking toward one of the actors, the bad guy. We used this cue because it was clearly distinguishable from other noises on stage but could not be heard by the audience. Ultrasonic bleepers are also quite useful as attention-getters when filming or photographing animals: I have used this technique to good effect not only with pets, but with animals in the wild and at zoos.

An anti-barking collar is now available that works on the same principle as the Aboistop, but it releases ultrasound, when the dog barks, from a unit worn around its neck. As one would expect, most dogs respond initially, but get used to the sound after a while. However, some remain sensitive and the device reliably interrupts their barking.

From the standpoint of animal welfare, it is unfortunately the case that technology has worked more to the disadvantage of animals than to their benefit. Personally, I am attracted to exploring the beneficial interface between science and animal welfare, and I always have an eye open for bringing the two together. Micro-electronics will, I am sure, find many more applications in the challenge of better dog training. For instance, it is feasible for vocal commands to be delivered by radio to a receiver unit that dogs can carry on their bodies. In return, the dog can wear a microphone, even a miniaturized TV camera, with a telemetric link back to a human to monitor the dog's behavior. Heart rate, blood pressure and the like can already be telemetrically monitored to ensure that the animal is not suffering undue distress while it is away from the trainer. These can sometimes be important issues, such as for a guide dog working in cities and confronted by noisy, polluting traffic.


## TOOTHBRUSH

The care of dogs' teeth is an important responsibility for owners, since we are the ones who have taken over their feeding, introducing unnatural diets that can have disastrous effects upon their oral health. The single most useful thing owners can do for their dogs' teeth is to clean them on a daily, even twice-daily basis. A specially designed soft toothbrush is very efficient at removing plaque, the organic matrix consisting of bacteria and food particles that adheres to the surface of the teeth. If you do not brush away this plaque, it is liable to become mineralized and form unsightly and smelly adhesions to the tooth. Look at your own dog's teeth, especially his canine and rear molar teeth (see diagrams on page 86). Do they suffer from a yellow discoloration? That is calculus, and you need to see your veterinary surgeon, who can remove it with specialized scaling equipment.

The process of brushing a dog's teeth helps create a positive and respectful relationship between you and your dog. It should become a high point of his day, as important as mealtimes and a massage. To be even more effective, use an anti-bacterial toothpaste specifically devised for dogs and cats, which can be purchased from veterinary surgeons and pet stores. Human toothpastes contain foaming agents and flavors that dogs dislike: they prefer meat to mint!

## FLASHLIGHT

Many of us are obliged to exercise our dogs in darkness during the winter months. It can be useful to train dogs to respond to simple visual signals from a flashlight at an early age, so that one can call one's dog in at dead of night from the neighbor's garden. I recommend that from puppy days onward the "come" signal as spoken and hand signal (see page 58) be linked to a flash, given at one-second intervals.

The problem of locating a dog in the dark is well known to Irish setter owners, whose dogs can "quarter" ground at incredible speeds and distance. A device I have found useful is a flashing battery-powered collar, which at least lets you know where the dog is roaming. It probably also provides a useful early warning to rabbits and other nocturnal creatures, who can thereby avoid unwelcome canine company.

## TOYS

The frustration of unaccompanied confinement to a kennel, a small house or life on a leash is the most widespread source of suffering for the contemporary dog. It matters not that a dog's kennel or backyard be one square yard, an acre or twenty acres, if it is not equipped with interesting and movable items to attract investigations and manipulation, the dog's imagination can only fade away. There are many practical measures to be taken to fight such frustration from boredom, among which are the purchase of appropriate toys. Let us look at what is available:

### Balls

Most dogs like to play ball, games of chase and retrieve when they are thrown by master or mistress. However, if left with a ball to play alone, most dogs rapidly tire: it is a focus for subject play, not object play, which maintains their interest. Bouncy rubber balls present a potentially serious danger because they can form a close-fitting plug in the dog's esophagus and choke him within minutes. A colleague of mine lost her full-grown German shepherd when it asphyxiated on a tennis ball someone had thrown for it. It was dead within minutes, despite her vain attempts to force the ball from its throat. The moral of the story is only to purchase balls that are too large for the dog to pick up easily and carry. Small balls of golf-ball proportions should simply be banned as unsafe for dogs. The material of which balls are constructed is important. Natural rubber is more difficult to tear than any of the composite materials widely employed in dog toys. Foam-filled toys are especially dangerous, since their contents can be swallowed and cause intestinal blockages as they expand in the stomach.

Some dogs love to chase and "kill" balls, especially footballs in the park. These are often dogs of high-drive breeds, like bull terriers, Staffies and boxers, dogs that just love to conquer. An American inventor, Joan Schultz, has devised an indestructible and safe harassment ball for these "conquistador" dogs, manufactured from non-toxic polyethylene. The balls are sized so that the dog can never pick them up, just dribble and chase them around. My experience of these Boomer balls is that they should be offered to ball-crazed dogs on a rationed and supervised basis, for five- to ten-minute workouts. The same design concept is now widely employed to enrich the lives of understimulated zoo, laboratory and farm animals.

## Digging pits

On a recent trip to western Canada, I was surprised to find that the most common complaint among callers to my radio and TV shows was that their dog dug up the garden, even burrowed under the foundations of houses. The breeds most likely to exhibit these behaviors were malamutes and huskies: spitz dogs closest to the sociable wolf and probably distressed by solitary confinement in their owners' yards, maybe trying to build a natural scrape or den.

My recommendation for these frustrated gardeners was again born of experience in dealing with zoo animals: to provide an artificial digging pit. The concept is quite novel in the world of dogs, but several of our clients at the Animal Behaviour Centre have now installed them, and all have given the concept their thumbs-up.

Construct a simple enclosure above ground, or a drained pit which can be filled with wood chippings. The latter are readily available from lumber yards and some garden centers, and are ideal because they are light and clean. The size needs to be matched to the size of the dog, but a guide would be to have a square pit with side lengths the nose-to-tail length of the dog, and of the same height. Sides can be constructed of wood, and are available in prefabricated form.

Teach your digging dog that this is the place where he may find buried food or other treasure, and thereafter scatter several big biscuits through the wood chips each day. Of course, he will flick chippings everywhere, but it is a simple chore to sweep and shovel them back. Only when you have provided this positive outlet can you discourage him from digging elsewhere in your garden. That might be discouragement with the can or, for a dog that dislikes water, running the hose into his other pits.

## Dumbbells

For training to retrieve, a variety of dumbbell designs and sizes are available to allow dogs to pick up comfortably. Ideally, select a design manufactured in soft materials such as rubber, wood or canvas.

## Frisbees

Frisbees have been all the rage among owners of agile dogs for more than a decade, and they can demand amazing aerial acrobatics from competitive canine catchers. They can also become an attractive part of social play between two humans and a dog. An important factor governing choice of Frisbee is that the plastic or other material of which it is constructed be soft and light, as heavy-construction Frisbees can cause slab fractures to the dog's teeth when grabbed at speed.

## Kong

Hunting is the skilled pursuit of the unpredictable, and it is the uncertainty about which way prey will turn that makes hunting such a good sport for dogs. These qualities of unpredictability have been designed into a very special kind of dog toy, the Kong, by an American dog-lover and engineer, Joe Markham. He was working on his Volkswagen when he noticed that his German shepherd was suddenly in wild pursuit of the shock absorbers. They were constructed from natural rubber, which bounced in an eccentric, unpredictable fashion.

Joe Markham extended the shock absorber concept into a series of shapes that produced the most dynamic movement, and perfected materials technology for molding and vulcanizing natural rubber into chew-resistant material. The choice of rubber was important for Joe Markham because his own dog had the bad habit of chewing stones, as do others which are bored and deprived of play opportunities. The Kong has a hollow interior that collapses under the strain of chewing, while its elastic rubber permits penetration of teeth into the Kong without puncturing.

At the Animal Behaviour Centre we find the Kong toy to be the most therapeutic device yet created to entertain dogs, be they at home or in kennels, with or without human company. The substitute stimulation of exciting object play is especially important for dogs in kennels, where the strangeness and stress of a featureless, lonely environment reliably precipitates abnormal, compulsive activity.

The danger of rubber balls is that they can become lodged in the mouth and choke the dog, but the Kong is designed so that this cannot occur. By its very nature, play leads to a lowering of the instinct for self-preservation, so safety should be the first priority. The manufacturers of Kong guarantee that they are irresistible, but in our experience at the Animal Behaviour Centre a few dogs become overstimulated and too wild during play with this device. For those individuals, play with the world's best dog toy just has to be rationed.

### Nylon chews

Given the destructive power of dogs' teeth, manufacturers of toys have constantly sought ever-tougher material to work with. Synthetic nylon has been molded into an assortment of shapes like bones, balls and Frisbees, and some dogs love to chew them if they are also prone to chewing other hard objects such as stones. However, because nylon lacks elasticity and does not bounce, most dogs find it boring. Nylon toys should never be thrown as they can induce slab fractures when grabbed at speed.

A derivative of this concept is a chew based on plasticized casein, which can be cooked and puffed in the microwave. My experience is that this is popular with dogs and is good for both their nutrition and their teeth.

## Ropes

Rough ropes made from the natural fibers of flax and cotton can make excellent toys for dogs. Unlike nylon, these natural products can be digested and cleared from the dog's gut if swallowed accidentally, and they permit penetration of the teeth and massage the gums. The loose, tufted ends of commercially made rope toys stimulate the same shake-kill action as when a wolf tears into its prey, or a terrier shakes a rat to dislocate the spinal cord of its victim. In the puppy playgroups that we run at the Animal Behaviour Centre, these rope toys are by far the favorite objects for social play, as they stimulate chase, "kill" and tug-of-war games between puppies.

There is some evidence that these ropes can function along the lines of dental floss, polishing the surface of the tooth and dislodging organic plaque and food debris.

## Squeakers

Enter any pet store and you will find counters overflowing with squeaky toys in plastic and latex rubber, in incredible shapes varying from the torsos of politicians to plucked chickens, vegetables and the more classic knuckle bones. Many are downright dangerous and can be fragile, easily punctured or swallowed. The squeaking mechanism in particular is a favorite object for ingestion by curious dogs anxious to "kill" the distress calls of a "prey." The only safe material for manufacturing such toys is natural rubber latex, but even these should only be offered under constant supervision and the toy removed if signs of wear or damage are spotted.

## Trash-inventive toys

You do not need a big budget to create a physically interesting and enriched environment. There are always materials in garbage cans that can be turned to the worthy cause of entertaining your dog. At the simplest, plastic drink-bottles make ideal toys, the crackling crunch response reliably eliciting excitement. However, be careful to supervise play with such fragile items and remove them as soon as loose edges or fragments of the material are detached.

Paper, especially cardboard, stimulates play in many dogs; again an excellent material, being soft, fibrous and non-toxic. Label such materials as toys by participating in the initial games yourself, after which your dog will probably continue playing with the same object alone. Many dogs love dangling objects to grab and hang on to, whether leather straps, rope hanging from a tree, or balls. For the really destructive macho chewer, a suspended car or bicycle tire can make an excellent, free, stretchy tug-toy.

Finally, the sport of agility has caught on throughout North America. The elements of an agility course are well known and all are easily made from trashed or secondhand materials. For instance, planks to construct seesaws and ladders for high-level walkways. The only limits are those of human imagination.

## Wood

Many dogs chew on wood and obtain great satisfaction from doing so. Wolves have been observed to do so in the wild, especially upon young shoots and emergent grasses. Such materials usually have a high sugar content and my own experience is that young willow shoots are preferred by carnivores, be they dogs, bears or big cats. The fibrous structure of willow does not splinter, which in most other timber can cause problems to the mouth of a dog.

Sticks casually collected on a walk can be a particularly dangerous play object and should never be thrown, as horrible injuries to the throat are caused when dogs run on to them. Always be selective about which wood materials you permit your dog to chew, and test for their splinter-forming potential on your own hands. Remember, a dog's gums are considerably more delicate than your hands!

Finally, bear in mind that any object in the environment may be selected by your dog and used as a toy, and it is your responsibility to protect him from those that are dangerous. The danger may be subtle: for instance sweetcorn husks are a particularly common cause of gastrointestinal blockage to dogs. But there are many more potential dangers from plastic, nylon, wood and stone.

## TRAINING CRATES

Call them crates, cages or pens, the idea of confining dogs at certain stages of training has become the normal way in North America, but is still regarded by some as a subtle means of torture in Britain and

Europe. On this subject, I am with the Americans! Training crates are the single most useful investment a puppy owner can make, after the can, after the extending leash! Crates enormously simplify the prevention of house soiling, they protect puppies from being stepped upon when they are small, from chewing electrical cables or taking poisons, and they condition juveniles to accept periods of separation from humans. They limit the physical damage that a panicky dog can do, preadapt dogs to the inevitable periods of confinement they might experience later at the veterinary surgeon's or boarding kennels, and provide a safe environment for dogs in transit, especially in the car where the risk of death from a traffic accident is only a second away. The uses of crates for problem prevention and problem solving are legion, and the time to make that investment is at the start, the moment puppy comes home.

In nature, wolves construct several dens, underground structures to provide shelter from the elements, protection from other predators and especially for when cubs are born. Throughout the summer these are often no more than rudimentary scrapes in soil or vegetation, but in winter they are usually more substantial structures, often burrowed beneath a large tree trunk. Wolves only flop out to sleep during hot weather as an adaptation to keep cool. In winter and at other times, sleeping and lying is a social and group affair, curled together in a heap. Thus, to be in an enclosed space for sleeping is a natural thing for dogs, and we should not look upon training crates as prisons, rather as dens.

There are many designs and materials used for the construction of puppy crates. Much depends upon the breed of dog you have, its likely tolerance of a crate when first confined (a tough adult dog can destroy most things) and how much space is available. My preference is for the open wire-mesh structures, the classic crate, so that you can see exactly what is going on inside and the dog has easy visual, chemical and tactile contact with humans and dogs outside. The more enclosed, extruded plastic crates may provide privacy and be suitable for shipping by airlines, but they are less suitable for puppy training if they place the animal in a state of sensory deprivation.

The sizing of crates is vitally important. Unfortunately there is no single and scientifically devised standard for the process, it all being a matter of best judgment by the "experts." Here, I will adopt the role of expert and make my own, personal recommendation for getting the size of crate to suit the breed of dog you have. First, the height must allow your dog to stand without lowering its head. If you have a Great Dane, that can mean a gigantic structure three feet high, which just might influence whether or not you go in for crate training. Then the length must be a minimum of one and a half times the core length of your dog's body, being nose to base of tail. The width must allow the dog to stretch out fully, i.e., it should equal the dog's height when standing, at the rump or shoulders.

What if you have a puppy, tiny in relation to his eventual adult proportions? Ideally you will have two or three sizes of crates, and puppy will graduate through the sizes as he grows up. That might injure your bank balance, unless you are as fortunate as members of the puppy playgroup at the Animal Behaviour Centre, where we rent out crates on a weekly basis during the phase of puppy growth, members purchasing the final size only if and when needed. Otherwise, there is no alternative but to purchase the size of crate you expect your puppy to need when he grows up.

The first introduction of a puppy, or adult dog, to the crate is vital if it is to be perceived as a natural and positive environment rather than a prison. Do leave the door open for the first day or so, and feed the dog inside. If you have a small child in the family, let him or her hop inside and create the image of the crate being a playpen. Make it comfortable and leave water. Only after this initial acceptance should the door be closed, still with increased rather than decreased human attention from the outside. I have proved this point very well with our puppy, Pollo, who accepted his crate immediately and hops into it as the natural and safe environment in which to sleep when the going gets rough with our cats, kids, or he is just exhausted. We need never worry that he might be delving into cupboards, fridges or rewiring the house, he cannot interfere with the burglar alarms nor, for that matter, can he bite the burglar! And very importantly, our aging Sam, who needs his peace and privileges, can take a break from the teasing attentions of Pollo.

Different sections of the problem-solving Part Three make reference to the use of crates in housebreaking puppies, and overcoming specific problems in adulthood such as when adult dogs are destructive. If the price tag of a regular and commercially constructed crate is daunting, there are many *ad hoc* DIY equivalents that can be put to the same purpose. There are tea chests for the youngest puppy, graduating to pole frames with wire stretched across, lashed together with baler cord. An area beneath a kitchen work surface, under the stairs or anywhere else that is easily visible but away from disturbance can be cordoned off as the dog den. All your dog needs is security, contact and a good view of humans in their world.


## VOICE

We all constantly talk to our pets, and I suggest that were we not to do so we would not be human, certainly not humane. Dogs respond to our tones of voice and maybe also to the content of our speech. Particular sounds or words can signal quite specific meanings. High emotion in human beings is associated with what speech researchers refer to as "strained intensity vocalization," where both voice box and larynx are contracted and sound is seemingly spat out. The early German dog trainers believed that it was helpful to "bark" commands at a dog rather than speak to them with an ordinary voice. Some dogs are certainly very responsive to tone of voice, becoming both distressed and attentive to an emotionally aroused voice. But then, dogs can detect human emotions by using their senses of smell (see page 15) and sight (by our nervous micromovements when aroused) as well as by the sound of our voices.

Then there is the issue of loudness when communicating with our dogs. Should we shout or should we speak? I am in no doubt that if we shout commands at a dog his sensitivity diminishes, committing us to an ascending spiral of noise if we are to cross the dog's boredom threshold. Better to cultivate attentive behavior in your pet and employ vocal commands that are of just sufficient intensity to rise above the background din.

A puppy can be quickly programmed to respond to our vocal language, but we need to keep it as simple and as consistent as possible. That's why it is vital to have a family consensus about the vocabulary employed to communicate with the dog. There is never a need to use voice as a punishment or unpleasant warning. Delegate that role to the rattle can, so that the voice is reserved for expressions of affection and as a carrier of information.

I've not mentioned upmarket booties, diapers, coats, costumes, perfume or jewelry for dogs. I am told by the famous London store, Harrods, that they were able to satisfy a gentleman who wanted to

purchase a $12,000 gold collar for his dog. But these are extrava-
gances that dogs cannot understand and may dread.

Dogs are not big-budget pets like horses. The countryside is awash
with good-quality nylon baler cord to braid into homemade collars
and leashes. Towns are littered with tin cans, and gentle kindness is
definitely yours for giving to dogs.

11

# Training Classes:
## *With Dogs in Mind*

Dog owners are fairly chummy types and it's good to get together with like-minded individuals. After all, we are social animals, so what could be more natural than joining a club that caters to both? Dog clubs and training classes are much in vogue, and some 40 percent of owners have joined one at some time, though not necessarily with their present pet. One wonders what the 40 percent were looking for compared to the 60 percent who have never been near training classes, and whether classes were useful to them.

An analysis of patients at the Animal Behaviour Centre revealed that 63 percent of the dogs that come to see us have attended training classes in the past, though most owners state that this was neither a productive nor even an enjoyable experience. The most common single failing of training classes seemed to be that too much emphasis was placed upon competitive obedience and insufficient emphasis upon the needs of the ordinary pet dog. It is always the high-speed Border collies and eager-to-please German shepherds that win the laurels, while the poodles, pugs and mutts have to make do as best they can.

Do dogs really benefit from training classes, or do clubs exist to satisfy the psychological needs of egotistical trainers rather than the behavioral needs of dogs? I am sure that at many of the clubs I have visited and lectured at, the criticism is justified and reform is overdue. However, I am equally convinced that there is a role for clubs that can benefit the canines, their human families and, most significantly of all, the wider community. However, my concept of a good training club differs from many of those already in existence, be they large, small, Kennel Club–registered or just private enterprises. This chapter is primarily for those who run or would like to run classes, though its contents may also be used as a consumer's guide to training clubs for owners who just want to train their pet with others.

## THE PURPOSE OF TRAINING CLASSES

The overriding objective for any club should be that it fulfills the needs of its members and has certain key priorities, including the following:

- To have fun (dogs and owners alike)
- To improve behavior (especially of dogs)
- To learn about dog care and behavior
- To improve the status of dogs in society
- To organize competitions involving dogs
- To balance the books (even make a small profit)

The order of the above-stated objectives reflects my own interests and prejudices about the subject, and for me the interests of dogs take precedence over other considerations. Too often, the priority of training clubs is for members to achieve a high degree of precision and speed in competitive exercises with their dogs. If, however, the purpose of the club is first to have fun and secondly to improve behavior, the competition side will be of less interest to the majority of its potential membership.

## THE PLACE FOR DOG TRAINING

The reader will have gathered by now that training never stops; a dog is constantly acquiring information and skills in a process which starts at birth and ends with his last gasp. A dog club has to meet somewhere, and too often in my experience it is in the local church or town hall, rented for the night and with the paraphernalia of the amateur

dramatic society, children's playgroup, poetry circle and others set to
one side. The main problem with such environments is that the pol-
ished floor surfaces are unsuitable; dogs slip, slide and become over-
concerned with maintaining balance. Then there is the issue of noise,
which can be of overwhelming importance in unfurnished, echoing
halls not fitted with absorbent drapes. Barking dogs naturally invite
people to raise their voices, so an ever-ascending cacophony tends to
ensue. Research shows that even in the modest range of between
eighty-five and ninety decibels, which is typical of traffic noise on a
busy street, dogs can suffer serious physiological and behavioral distress. Sound intensities at many of the training classes I have visited
are well in excess of that level.

A further handicap in most training venues is that dogs need to
communicate chemically and receive important information through
their noses. If the hall does not belong to the dog club, there tends to
be a constant concern about suppressing urine marking and disguising
the occasional Fido-mark with foul-smelling disinfectants. Together
with the artificial scents in floor polish, dogs at many training classes
inhabit an olfactory dustbin.

These criticisms can be easily overcome by meeting outdoors on
grass, cinder or tarmac. Only a minority of British dog training clubs
meet on such outdoor surfaces, and the excuse usually given is our
climate. In the U.S., Australia, and South Africa, where I have visited
and watched outdoor clubs, I see less stress for the dogs and more fun
for their owners. The British should not use their weather as an
excuse; on a recent trip to Iceland I visited a training facility perched
on a clifftop, with no protection from the prevailing Arctic winds.
When this comfort-conscious author expressed his amazement, it was
explained that people just dress up for the weather and keep moving
in winter. That is an admirable approach because dogs don't seem to
mind the cold.

Then there is the matter of space. Indoor halls tend to be Lilliputian in
scale, yet dogs like to run in free play. Cost considerations usually mean
that sufficient space can only be found in outdoor paddocks, though
some indoor equestrian centers possess covered schooling arenas on a
moss or wood-chip base, which is exceptional for dog training. But
where do you find a field, let alone an equestrian center, in one of our
large cities? The solution is often to negotiate with an organization that
owns vacant land, maybe a building developer who would be pleased to
see it fenced and producing an income. A dog trainer in Notting Hill,

London, has established a club that meets underneath the arches of an elevated highway, the M40. Vicki Carr's classes are very popular: the club helps to foster a sense of civic pride in this extraordinary environment which is hedged in on one side by a railroad line, on the other by graffitied pillars supporting the road above. Because her dog group runs litter patrols and picks up after the dogs, they set a good example to local children and would-be litterbugs.

The problem with grass is that it can be slippery and muddy after rain. On the other hand, large areas of pavement or concreted areas are not so easy to find and can be unpleasant, even dangerous for dogs to run, jump and occasionally fall upon. Various artificial surfaces have been created for human sports and maybe a doggy-version of all-weather astroturf needs to be tried out.

More practical than natural or artificial grass are loose-laid blocks or bricks with soil and grass in between which can be ideal venues for dog training, especially if they also have lighting. Then there are the neighbors to be considered in the choice of a site.

## THE TIME FOR TRAINING

It is well-known that dogs adopt sleep–activity rhythms that broadly mirror our own, be they diurnal with peak activity in daytime or a crepuscular rhythm with active mornings and evenings. They are creatures of habit, so try to go to training classes at a time when your dog is at his most active. Evening classes are not suited to the dog who usually has an after-dinner nap at this time. Having run training groups in both daytime and the evening, I can attest to the definite advantages of the former. Natural daylight helps you to see the dogs' movements more clearly, and all concerned can keep a lookout for potential danger. If need be, conduct weekend classes to accommodate the needs both of dogs and of their owners who work through the week.

## THE PEOPLE: SELECTION, TRAINING AND STYLES FOR TRAINERS

A common stereotype of dog trainers is that they are big, brash, usually male, more the commander than the teacher. In reality, increasing numbers of women are involved in dog training and many of those I meet have good communication skills. The first prerequisite of a good teacher is that he or she be an attentive listener, understanding the needs and signs of pupils. He or she must tailor the message to the audience, involve them, make them feel important and focus as much upon those who have difficulty following instructions as upon those who excel.

But where can these skills be acquired? The ideal dog training instructor will be a qualified teacher, because the principles of good teaching work as well upon an audience of children as upon a crowd of dog owners. Then again, there are courses organized by various institutes, by the Kennel Club, by myself at the Animal Behaviour Centre and others. However, there is no substitute for experience or the advantage of possessing a naturally interesting and warm personality. Some have the qualities needed to make good teachers; others do not.

In training groups with which I am connected, we demand that voices never be raised and that conversational tones be used. An instructor should not offend the sensitivities of his audience by references to their race, sex or physical characteristics. It is too easy to raise a cheap laugh with sexist jokes or focus conversational banter upon an owner who has difficulty with his dog.

The worst crime of all is to pass public judgment on an owner. I have had a client come to me in tears after harsh words from a dog trainer about a constantly barking Jack Russell. On a previous occasion at the classes, the poor dog had been attacked by another dog and his barking was part of a wider nervous–defensive behavior. Eventually, my client was asked to leave the classes, an all-too-frequent experience for nonconformist dogs in training clubs. Remember, the first objective should always be that training is fun. Individuals having difficulties with their dogs can be taken aside and advised on a one-to-one basis, always treated with respect.

## COMMITTEES AND CONSTITUTIONS

Most dog-training clubs are run as charities, with little interest in the profit motive. That can work well, so long as someone has good leadership skills and is supported by a hardworking committee and enthusiastic members. Even charities need good administration, so the club will need a constitution, a committee, and adherence to democratic procedures. It is always worth having a clearly defined statement of objectives for the club, short enough to be memorable and certainly no more than a single paragraph. For instance: "The East Hythe dog-training club exists to promote good behavior in dogs, to improve the appreciation and facilities for dogs in the East Hythe community and to organize enjoyable leisure pursuits involving dogs and their owners."

## ACTIVITIES

Training dogs is obviously the core activity of a club, but as you will have gathered, I believe training to be mostly an individual affair, taking only minutes if the methodology is correctly selected to match the needs of the dog. Although most training is best conducted with man and dog alone there are some things better done in groups and none is more important than play. What follows is a list of dog-related activities that can be intelligently modified according to the numbers, environment and ambitions of club members.

### Social play

The general concept of dogs coming together and playing is often referred to as socialization, a rather loose and overused term. What I aim for is free interaction between dogs with light management from humans. Some dogs seem to find boisterous play with another dog frightening, others threatening, and for a minority, free play is just too stimulating. During the first few moments of play, owners may therefore have to intervene. I suggest that debutants be restrained on an extending leash while selected, predictable dogs come forward to make their acquaintance. The possibility of a fight is ever present and safety equipment should therefore always be to hand: an aerosol alarm, a compressed $CO_2$ fire extinguisher, water, blankets, a light board to place between threatening dogs and the like. During social play, little interest will usually be directed at either objects or humans. Play sessions should both precede and terminate the training phase of the meeting and need not last more than five minutes.

## The attentive line

While I do not believe it desirable that dogs parade in a circle around a trainer, it is still worthwhile having dogs do things for their owners in the company of strange dogs and people. As the title attentive line suggests, the first exercise should be walking and heeling in a straight line, deviating neither forward, back nor to the side. Terminate with the "sit" about three feet from another dog and facing it, either as a pair or a small circle of six to eight dogs. This procedure is a good exercise in restraining the natural tendency of dogs to rush forward and investigate their fellow canines.

## Multi-handler experience

The idea of swapping dogs is quite alien to many dog trainers; indeed some clubs stipulate that only one person be allowed to train the family dog in classes. Nothing could be more damaging to the dog; he should learn to receive direction from a variety of humans so long as they are all competent and physically able to manage him. People have to be matched to other dogs in the class and introduced, so that they get to know both the strange dog and its owner. Training classes can therefore provide the basis for friendship formation between humans as much as between dogs. From control comes respect, and breeds prone to form overprotective attachments to their owners seem to benefit particularly from this process of round-robin introductions to strangers.

## Social graces

Normal human etiquette demands that there are occasions when one just cannot pick one's nose or scratch one's crotch. There is a time and a place for everything! So it is with dogs, and one function of training classes can be to sharpen the social graces. For instance, you can persuade your dog not to jump up on strangers by applying the tin-can-interruption technique (see page 114). Then again, you may wish to train a dog to stop barking in social situations (see page 126). Dogs can be trained to lie down at such times, not in a harsh aggressive way but in a relaxed position that does not interfere with discourse between humans.

## Chase tests

Too many dogs chase runners or joggers, and training classes can be the ideal environment to overcome this problem. Simply place the dogs at intervals across the training ground in a sit or possibly down posture and have one or more people jog through them. If a dog rises to chase, the jogger should stop while the owner reinstitutes the sit posture, enforced if necessary with the rattle can. At worst, a chase or actual attack upon the jogger can be punished by throwing cans in the direction of the canine miscreant.

## The examination

No, I do not mean SAT examinations for dogs, but subjecting them to the kind of physical examination that they might receive at the vet's. This can be extended into a more formal show-stand posture, with examination of teeth, testicles, limbs and the like. Ensure that the dogs are rewarded with tidbits after undergoing their examination.

## Agility

From small and fun-orientated beginnings in the 1970s, agility has grown into a competitive, organized sport where some participants are liable to take themselves too seriously.

Not all dogs want to jump; some are unsteady on heights or show no aptitude for high-speed chasing. If the equipment is set up in the exercise area, club members can opt in or out of particular apparatuses and activities. Small, fat dogs are at a disadvantage to lean, tall, athletic types. Although the latter could be regulated by a system of handicaps, Border collies almost always seem to end up winning!

## Scent work

The basic methodology for teaching dogs to locate and retrieve objects by scent was given in Chapter 6 (page 67). It should always be a fun-orientated task, which may not be easy to teach in the environment of a training club. Under Kennel Club rules, a standardized scent-discrimination test is prescribed, where the dog identifies one of several "marked" with either the owner's or the judge's odor.

I propose a more complex and interesting task in which objects are hidden from view and located by their smell. In many respects, this can be more easily taught to a group of dogs by another trained dog than by a person (see page 52).

### The chorus line

Howling is the signal for reunions and departures by both wild and domestic canids; it is a contact call that can have a strong emotional content. A communal howling session can be the high spot on which to end training sessions as it can also be a great advertising call to residents of the neighborhood. One accomplished canine chorister is needed to lead the singing, then others in the group should join in. Of course, there may always be some who will not!

### Lectures

There should be a learning component for the owners of dogs attending training clubs. A mini-series of lectures or tutorials can be arranged around topics which interest or concern the group, and I make some suggestions here:

• Feeding dogs
• Birth control
• Equipment
• The law
• Ethics and animal rights
• Veterinary emergencies
• Worms and zoonoses
• Wild dogs and the history of domestication
• The work of animal charities
• Dogs and blood sports
• Community care

These teaching sessions can be the principal vehicle for showing owners a better way to train their dogs. More important than training dogs to perform particular tasks is the overall philosophy or attitude to training. The general approach explained in earlier chapters of this book can be emphasized, such as the need to exploit existing response-tendencies and obtain instrumental control over dog behavior rather than to teach them unnatural "tricks." I envisage twenty to thirty minutes for each lecture session, with another thirty minutes for practical fun sessions involving the dogs. After that, matters can take a social turn by opening the bar!

## Puppy playgroups

Many dog training clubs insist that animals reach a minimum age before they join, six to nine months being typical. Of course, others appreciate that this is a ludicrous restriction, which is why puppy playgroups are such a good concept. My experience at the Animal Behaviour Centre is that playgroups usefully involve more than just a single age group. As well as puppies there should be some adult dogs around, because they provide a stabilizing influence. That has certainly been the role of our two linchpin canines Sam and Jasper, one a sophisticated show-off, the other a playful hooligan. To have an effective playgroup also requires a diverse environment such as a farm, where there is easy access to other domesticated animals. Of course, adult dogs that may traumatize puppies by behaving aggressively or simply by throwing their weight around, should be kept apart from puppies.

A minimum and probably critical number of ten puppies is required to make the concept work. Fewer than that and there is insufficient choice offered to the canine participants, but more than fifteen and the group can degenerate into chaos. Essentially the same exercises apply for puppies as for adults, with a strong focus upon multi-person handling, tidbit reward from strangers, teaching owners methods for exploiting the follow (i.e., "come") response and other procedures outlined in Chapters 6 and 7.

## Equipment

Many training classes are run in cooperation with a nearby pet store that stocks the equipment members will require for their dogs. They will obviously need the correct collars and leashes, toys, dumbbells, tidbits and the like. Everything that is needed is described in Chapter 8. It goes without saying that choke chains simply should not be available to members of a well-run training club if animal welfare has any priority. It would, however, be sensible for collars and leashes to be inspected for safety by someone who is competent in these matters, because weak, worn or excessively narrow collars can be dangerous.

An alternative to cooperation with the local pet store is for the club to market directly equipment that it believes to be necessary and beneficial to the dogs' behavior. The profit from such sales can either be directed at maintaining or improving facilities for the whole club or distributed to worthy canine and human charities. The economics of this largesse from club funds is made possible by the substantial discounts that can be negotiated with pet accessory wholesalers if you buy on behalf of the club.

Finally, a health warning from a reformed smoker. The evidence of dangers from secondary smoking is now so persuasive that cigarette smoking in public places should be regarded as anti-social not only for humans, but for dogs as well. Aside from the polluting effects of tobacco smoke, dogs can be burned by cigarettes as owners fumble in training. *Ban them!* The polluting effects of cigarette smoke not only interfere with a dog's physical health, but also with his behavior by blocking the sense of smell. Think of the beagles.

The training class I have outlined here is like nothing that exists except perhaps at the Animal Behaviour Centre. I wish there were more, because real friendships are struck between fellow members of the club and with me and my colleagues. We do have the benefit of the farm around which to stroll, but that might also be available to other clubs who situate themselves in a field. After that, comfortable chairs, reliable heating and a well-stocked bar ensure that dog training really can be fun.

Please note that there has been no suggestion of certificates or rosettes being awarded for participating in classes. There need not be upper and lower classes, passes or failures, nor any reward other than just being in good company. Some will find this lack of competition a frustrating omission from my ideal training club. I try to encourage such people to take up another pursuit to fulfill their competitive urges, rather than one that involves dogs.

Part Three

# BEHAVIORAL THERAPY FOR PROBLEM DOGS

Few of us will admit to owning a problem dog, as indeed few parents take kindly to a teacher referring to their child as a problem pupil. Our pets are, after all, part of the family and we love them despite their foibles and shortcomings. From time to time, though, the behavior of dogs can really get out of hand, and when complaints are received or writs begin to fly, who can you turn to for help? In this section, I will provide recipes for solving the most common canine behavioral problems.

Dogs are not like peas from a pod and therapy appropriate for one animal may be inappropriate for another with superficially similar symptoms: it is not the dog but the method that is wrong when it fails to respond to a therapeutic procedure. If you are in doubt about what to do about your pet's behavior and confused by a maze of conflicting advice from Tom, Dick, Harry and Roger, consult your veterinary surgeon. Most vets have had some training in animal behavior as part of their university degree, and a good many take a particular interest in the subject. Many will have attended courses or lectures by myself and other specialists and will be flattered that you have thrown the challenge of your pet before them. A vet is also the logical person from whom to seek help about behavior, because many behavioral disturbances have a clinical cause. Fully six out of ten of the canine patients who come to the Animal Behaviour Centre either present odd and unwanted behaviors which are a symptom of some underlying medical state, or require a medical approach to treating the behavior. Most of the cases that are referred to our Centre are certainly well beyond the diagnostic resources of the average dog training club.

The first step in tackling any unwanted behavior in your dog is to investigate its underlying cause: what is the function of the behavior in the wild, and how has this tendency developed in your pet? What options are open to you? It may be helpful to list some of them:

• Do nothing: put up with it
• Modify the behavior
• Avoid the problem: change lifestyle, leave home!
• Rehome the dog with a neighbor, a friend or a charity
• Euthanatize the dog

In other words, how far are you prepared to go? Compare the overall seriousness of your pet's problems with the positive attractions that he brings to you and to your family. These latter almost always outweigh the negatives, especially if you recall the small number of occasions on which the problem has arisen and express that as a percentage of your total time together.

An important quality needed for successfully tackling the treatment of behavioral problems is optimism: a certainty that you can deal with it and that canine behavior is not cast in an immutable mold. Believe me, there is never a time when dogs stop learning, and many of the therapies that we employ produce dramatic results within minutes.

In this section, I will look at the common problems. We begin with aggression, the most important and demanding issue of them all.

# 12
# Canine Aggression

If your dog bites, the victim can face serious medical hazards; there are also legal liabilities and not a little emotional upset and fear. Always bear in mind that aggression is not a unitary concept and that there are several types of aggression, which all have different causes and symptoms. There is no one approach to treating it and you will need to be skillful and well-read to understand why it occurs. You may already have noticed that your dog is only aggressive in fairly specific conditions—he may bite the letter carrier at the door but not other visitors or letter carriers away from home, or he may get wildly excited by the sight of people outside the car but is tolerant when they are passengers inside. Contrary to popular belief, problems of aggression do not usually have their origins in the dominance of either dog or owner. Many people are bitten because their pet loves them too much, is frightened, or is in pain.

## AGGRESSION TO OWNER AND FAMILY

It is particularly upsetting for the hand that feeds a dog to be bitten: there is a sense of betrayal that your best friend could do this to you, and a loss of trust. The warning signs may have been given but you couldn't believe that your dog would actually bite. Your first priority should be to ensure that no one is bitten again, so you must refrain from physically taking on, punishing or confronting your dog until a clear strategy has been thought through, discussed with others in the household and put to the test. If you strike out at the dog in rage, you will probably not achieve any constructive objectives and could well end up being badly bitten. Depending on the cause of the problems, these are some of the treatment scenarios you should contemplate.

## The competitive dog

Maybe there is some power struggle between you and your dog, especially if there seems to be a policy of divide and rule, where certain people are obeyed, others are threatened or symbolically "walked" over. Fortunately, the rules whereby dogs manipulate social situations are well-researched and can be modified by some or all of the following measures. These are specific and usually short-term rearrangements for competitive and potentially dangerous dogs and would not be necessary for the majority of dogdom.

*Keep a height advantage.* Do not allow the competitive dog on chairs or beds as this brings him to your level, and height reinforces social rank. If who sleeps where becomes an issue, exclude the dog from your bedroom, even from going upstairs.

*Don't be pushed around.* If the pushy dog initiates any activity, even friendship, ignore it. Later, you can command that he come, then sit, then is stroked at a time that suits you, but not necessarily at a time determined by the dog.

*Enforce every command.* You will know from past experience whether or not your dog has heard and understood a command, and once should be enough. If he ignores you, first get his attention with the rattle can and then repeat with more emphasis upon the command.

*Handle the dog.* Use the massage technique explained on page 42, give a daily clinical examination for fleas, muck in his ears or an injured paw, and finish off with a tooth brushing session.

*Games are serious.* Don't let your dog win or even begin tug-of-war games. Rough-and-tumble play that allows him to stand on top of you communicates the wrong message about who is in control.

Better to play managed games, such as sit, throw an object and then permit him to run out and fetch. Chase games are fine so long as they terminate at a time and a place determined by you, not by the dog.

*Obedience.* Regular obedience is important in a dog that tries to take over from time to time. Work in areas where you are likely to succeed, away from distractions, perhaps in an enclosed garden. An obedience class with slippery floors and yapping dogs is definitely not the best place for you or your dog to learn. Under no circumstances send your dog away to be trained by a "professional": you must make the investment of time and effort in your own dog.

*Walk ahead.* The dog that pulls is in control and it is important that he follows you, the leader. If you are encountering difficulties, use a halter and an extending leash as described on page 122.

*Diet.* Indulgent, human-type food may cement the human-companion animal bond, but it also makes you a potential competitor to your dog. Better to remove any suspicion that you are "stealing" his rations by feeding him a boring dry food, at times and in places away from the human family's meals. Ensure there are no more table scraps nor rewards for begging.

*Hormones.* It is more likely that there will be competitive aggression with a male dog than with a female. Depending upon the overall behavioral profile, castration reliably reduces that type of aggression. Indeed, if you have a dog of a breed known for its assertive and sometimes violent tendencies it is better to castrate before puberty, say at four to five months of age. Synthetic hormones of the progestogen family available from veterinary surgeons, can be a useful adjunctive treatment for some macho dogs.

*Be careful.* Don't seek unnecessary confrontation, and if you have to do something to your dog that is unpleasant for it, put a basket muzzle on him (see page 124).

*Crisis-intervention.* Even the best-laid plans go wrong and you must be able to protect yourself with a rattle tin can or aerosol alarm at high-risk moments.

*Role playing.* If your dog only persecutes one or two members of the family but is nice to others, the latter should conscientiously ignore him, thereby increasing his motive to find friendship and leadership from those he is victimizing.

*Teeth.* The damage from dog bites is always from the four big canine teeth, which has led American veterinarians and ourselves at the Animal Behaviour Centre to explore a new orthodontic procedure. Briefly, the height of the canine teeth is reduced to the level of the surrounding incisors and premolars, at which level they cannot cause much damage. Strangely, dogs that have received this disarming procedure become less likely to seek confrontation, probably because their prospective victims behave in a more confident fashion. This is still a relatively new technique, even for veterinarians with specialist training in dentistry.

## The possessive dog

Some dogs only bite their owners when food or some treasured object is around: they are possessive. It may be an inherently attractive item such as a bone or food bowl, but often it can be an intangible or apparently pointless resource such as tissue paper, socks, even a person. Cocker spaniels are especially prone to becoming possessive of places such as under chairs, of people, or of things. Badly timed punishment can dramatically worsen such behaviors, and you should proceed more thoughtfully as follows:

*Devalue the object.* Market forces affect the behavior of dogs as much as people: a resource in plentiful supply has a lower perceived value than one that is scarce. Thus, if the dog defends tissue paper, increase the supply. If it guards food, increase rations and supply it in many bowls, several meals a day.

*Avoidance.* Certain problems are more easily avoided than confronted: There is no reason why dogs should have bones, so simply exclude them from your pet's menu. If by some mischance your competitive dog finds a skeleton in the garden or a carcass in the woods, walk away and ignore him.

*Trade with your dog.* A definite option with object- and food-possessive dogs is to offer an item which is of greater "value" than that which he is defending. Simply put, if he wants to defend a bowl of medium-palatability food, offer a morsel of a more palatable ration in exchange. The owner then becomes associated with a process of reward through trade, rather than as a competitor to be challenged.

*Distract.* It is always best to change the context of confrontation, moving to a place or an environment where you stand the best chance of "winning" repossession of whatever your pet has. If a dog might be violent, stealing something in the house is usually best tackled by rattling the lead before going outside to call him. If caught in the act of some misdemeanor, use the rattle tin can or an aerosol alarm at that precise moment of wrongdoing.

*Punishment is out.* There is ample evidence that if you punish a dog for gaining possession of an object, fear makes violence more rather than less likely. The practical message is obvious.

Finally, beware an object- or food-possessive dog in the company of children and pay special attention to the danger of a child trying to regain possession of a toy or snack.

### The fearful dog

A few dogs are actually afraid of their owners. Some will have been through the old-fashioned dog training mill with its overemphasis on violent enforcement. Sometimes, however, the source of the underlying fear rests in mischance or bad luck. Perhaps someone accidentally trod on the dog or touched inflamed ears and provoked a defensive reaction. More likely, he had a deprived puppyhood and was under-socialized to people. It is difficult to give good general advice for what is certain to be a highly individual issue, but the following general strategies usually apply:

*Response-substitution therapy.* This technique was outlined on page 52, whereby we create a new behavior in a context that is incompatible with the expression of fearful or defensive reactions. For instance, wind the dog up into boisterous play with his favorite toy, or set him sternly into a sit or down posture before examining him in a sensitive area. You can then give a command or induce a position from which it will be impossible for him to withdraw.

*Desensitize.* Present the fear-evoking stimulus at low intensity, repeatedly for as long as it is tolerated. Gradually increase the intensity of the stimulation as it is progressively accepted, associating it with reward rather than with further stress. Always work within the tolerated limits of the dog.

*Check out the cause.* Your pet's nervous reactions may have some medical basis, so have your vet examine him.

*Happy-go-lucky attitude.* The good-humored attitude usually helps bring the withdrawn and defensive dog out of his shell: try not to show excessive sympathy for your fearful pet.

*Safety first.* Certain procedures must be conducted for the dog's own safety; grooming, nail-clipping or the dressing of a wound. In such circumstances, ensure your safety by muzzling the dog, or better, quietly restrain him with a halter.

### Problem prevention

Most forms of aggression toward members of the dog's own household can be prevented by following these simple rules:

1. Select the right breed for your circumstances.
2. Establish clear and effective rules of management from the earliest puppy days.
3. Involve all family members in care and training.

### AGGRESSION TOWARD VISITORS AND OTHER STRANGERS

Most people regard it as a bonus that dogs bark and have a clear concept of home territory. We hope that that approximates to the land we rent or own and that he won't stray beyond our house and garden. Remarkably, most of our pets do form that territorial concept, but a few go just too far in pursuit of strangers. The expression of territorial behavior in dogs can usually be changed by a simple process of learning: for instance the discovery by the dog that invasion from visitors brings food rather than bad experiences. In practice, this aspect of aggressive behavior is one of the most straightforward and reliable to modify using the following general plan:

*Safety first.* You can't take risks with other people's fingers, so if there is a risk, or a history of your dog having bitten people, muzzle him (see page 124).

*Create a positive handicap.* If your dog always barks and attempts to bite at the front door, begin trial introductions away from the place of greatest risk. Ask your more courageous friends to meet the dog either outside his territory or indoors. With many German shepherds of my acquaintance, they are fine when they first encounter visitors sitting in the living room or on the street, but are dangerous at the front door.

*The owner–dog emotional umbilicus.* You may not have realized you shared one of these with your pet, but it is true! The more rejecting and physically distant you are from your pet, the more motivated he or she will be to make friends with outsiders. If you are expecting someone to visit, make a point of not showing any emotional or vocal contact with your dog in the fifteen to thirty minutes before their arrival.

*Victim psychology.* There is ample evidence that some people are bitten a lot and are somehow predisposed to bring out the worst in other people's dogs. It may be chemical factors (pheromones), jerky movements of the hands and arms or a tendency to stare at dogs when frightened. Tone of voice unquestionably gives a clue to people's emotional state. Discourage visits in the early stages of therapy from those who express a definite fear of dogs, and concentrate upon those who are calm and claim to like them.

*Bribery buys friendship.* The payoff of a few tidbits secreted in deep pockets usually creates a powerful positive expectation in dogs. Tasty handouts can initially be tossed at the dog or popped through the mail slot. Dogs soon realize that visitors can actually be nicer to know than regular members of the household.

*The penalty.* Consider carefully before using any form of punishment, but what punishment there is must never be attributed to the visitor. A thrown tin can from the owner might be sufficient, but I have achieved some remarkable "cures," where intense barking is part of the overall territorial response, using the Aboistop smell-conditioning system (see page 127). Seemingly, by suppressing barking with the surprise smell of citronella, one can also suppress the rest of the territorial sequence.

*Response-substitution therapy.* It is as well to train your dog to lie down on a particular spot, within sight but out of reach of the front door or wherever else he is aggressive. This can be made a pleasurable response by the payoff of food, affection and other bounties.

Of course, problems of aggression toward strangers do not occur if owners follow my advice about multi-handler training in puppy days. Have all and sundry come to visit when your animal is young and you will not experience these problems. Some breeds are much more territorial than others, notably German shepherds. This has its roots in the sensitivity and nervousness of the breed, and their tendency to form powerful attachments to members of the family. Make a point of walking such a dog on open spaces away from home and occasionally recruit other dog walkers to hold his leash. He who holds the leash assumes symbolic control, and out of control comes first respect, later affection.

## FIGHTING DOGS

As was poetically pointed out to me by a biologist friend, "Carnivores don't have big teeth just to pick mushrooms!" They serve many functions, including negotiations with others of the same species. Occasional, ritualized fights with threats more than bites are a normal habit of any dog, but unfortunately some become skilled pugilists and neither acknowledge nor respond to appeasing and aggression-diverting signals from other dogs. Nothing is more certain to develop the skill of fighting than victory. To have a fighting dog makes its owner the pariah of the local dog-walking community. The more others avoid you with their pets, and you them, the less social your dog will become.

In our practice, the treatment of dogs aggressive toward other dogs attracts the highest success rate of all the common behavioral problems we see: 92 percent. The method is straightforward, does not require great skill and gives rapid results.

*Safety first.* You cannot let your dog cause mayhem in the local community, so restrain him on an extending leash, probably attached to a halter. If he is a really serious fighter, also fit a muzzle.

*School tolerance.* Dogs are strangely sensitive to "face." An embarrassment in front of another dog is as powerful a punishment as any. With your dog semi-free but controlled on a Flexi–Halti combination, walk in the vicinity of other dogs. Ideally, you will have a trained "stooge" dog who avoids eye contact with my threatening patient. Each time your dog raises his hackles, directs a stare, growls or, worse, lunges forward to attack, gently move his head sideways to break eye contact. Practice the technique in your own garden before setting out to the local park, where a mistake might cause injury to someone else's pet.

*Data collection.* Make a list of the dogs your pet likes rather than dislikes. Is yours a dog that mostly hates other males? Is it only big dogs, dogs of his own breed, or little yappy dogs? This profile will help you understand your dog's motives, which in most cases is that of competitive aggression between strange males.

*Sex and the surgeon.* If you find that your male dog only attacks other males, castration is a high priority. In addition, hormonal therapy might be offered by your veterinary surgeon, both before castration (as a partial predictor of how your dog might behave after the operation) and afterward to enhance the effects of neutering. If you want to avoid the possibility of your male dog becoming a fighter, have him neutered while he is young.

*Reward good behavior.* Your voice and overall attitude are the most significant factors which will encourage initial acceptance of strange dogs, even dogs that have previously suffered attacks. Later, the payoffs of play and the pleasures of sniffing interesting private parts of other dogs can take over from warlike tendencies.

*Punish the pugilists?* There is little role for conventional punishment in treating inter-male aggression; especially if this involves yanking on a choke chain. In practice, well-timed distraction of the earliest threats with a sound alarm may be helpful, or with the tin can if your pet has been sensitized to it (see page 114). If barking is an important part of the overall threat–attack sequence, disruption using the Aboistop (see page 127) can also be helpful. The look of surprise from a dog whose barky first threat suffuses him in the misty aroma of citronella is a delight to see.

*Patience makes perfection.* Don't imagine that success will come from just meeting one or two dogs a day; massed trials with twenty or more dogs per day should be the objective. You have to compensate for a relatively overprotected, dog-free existence you have previously imposed, so it is much better that you throw your dog in at the deep end.

*Clubbers of the world unite?* You may be fortunate enough to have a dog-training club near you that is run out of doors with a free-and-easy handling method. This can be a very therapeutic environment for reforming recalcitrant fighters. However, if the class is an indoor one on slippery floors and with trainers who shout "Leave!," you would be better off trying to find the solution at home.

*Voice and emotions.* You can communicate much of your intent and expectations through your voice, so stay calm and talk in "sweetie-pie," semi-juvenile tones.

The problem of dogs fighting is distressingly common and easily avoided if the basic social instincts of the dog are continuously exercised: early puppy experiences and daily walks should bring pleasurable contact with the local canine fraternity.

### SIBLING RIVALRY

An only dog can be a lonely dog, so I usually encourage keeping several dogs in the human pack if conditions are suitable. However, there can be penalties to having several dogs and the most harmonious families can have the occasional bicker, even a full-scale row. The more similar the personalities of the dogs involved, the more likely it is that there will be disputes. By far the worst combination would be to have same-sex littermates living together: two brothers or sisters sharing similar physique and temperament make it difficult for them to develop distinctive personalities and a natural rank order.

Our human instincts are usually to be democratic in our treatment of pets, but this can interfere with their acquisition of distinctively different social statuses and usually increases competition between them. We make matters worse by favoring the "underdog," a policy that always creates a focus for conflict and jealousy from the more assertive individual of the pair. In my experience, some of the most ferocious fights occur when two familiar dogs fight one another in the home.

Very often it is the much-loved humans who are the focus for a fight, perhaps just one person in the dog's life. Peace can reign as soon as that person leaves home. In other cases, dogs fight over something seemingly trivial and bizarre: a sock, a dead insect or a race to bark at the front door. Not only are sibling rivalries dangerous for the dogs, they are also extremely dangerous for humans who try to separate them. The first priority must be safety.

*Safety first.* If fights have been serious and caused wounds, both dogs should be muzzled for at least a week while the dangers and prospects are reviewed. Other useful safety hints are:

Trailing leashes attached to their collars, so that dogs can be grabbed and separated with less risk of bites.

A bucket of water, or a large tank outdoors into which scrapping dogs can be dunked. Sometimes it can be useful to have a flat board that can be used to break visual contact between the combatants.

An aerosol alarm, even a $CO_2$-based fire extinguisher, a blanket to throw over the dogs and other such *ad hoc* devices may be needed to separate fighting dogs.

But do be careful, as we can all become reckless when trying to save our loved pets from injuring one another.

*Keep them together.* Try not to separate the dogs more than is necessary, since the first seconds of a reunion are also usually the most dangerous. Try to develop a bond between them during play and walks together.

*The gonad connection.* If it is two males fighting, one of the pair should most definitely be castrated. In some instances, a hormonal therapy can be useful in further diminishing the masculine status of the underdog. It is generally wrong to castrate the initiator of fights; he may well be the logical alpha or top dog. The long-term objective is always to increase the social distance between fighting pairs.

In females, the probability of fights occurring at the beginning of estrus, and later at the onset of a phantom pregnancy, are usually higher than at other times. Remember that in wolf packs, reproduction is the prerogative of the alpha dog and you should keep careful records to see if there are changes in the liability to fight with the stage of her estrus cycle. There may then be good reasons to spay one or both of the fighting dogs.

*Dominance-suppression.* You will need to be stricter in demanding complete obedience from both dogs, because you can thereby suppress their taking initiatives and making threats against one another.

*Detective work.* Records of the times and places when fights occur will probably reveal a predictable pattern. Only one person may be present; it may just be a knock at the door or the telephone ringing that sets them off. It is obviously important to avoid these situations, or at least to modify practice to the extent necessary. Since fights are so often focused upon a favorite person in the household, one could jokingly suggest a tactical rehousing unless the dog's idol promises to become more aloof and less affectionate.

It is sometimes said that scrapping dogs should be allowed to get on with it, that they will somehow "sort themselves out." Unfortunately, that is a very dangerous strategy indeed, and I have seen tragic cases where dogs literally fought to the death. If the risk of two large dogs fighting is too great, sadly, rehoming of one must be considered, if only for the safety of humans. Consider too the chronic stress suffered by dogs experiencing alternate bouts of affection and conflict: They will be better living apart.

# 13
# Attachment Problems:
## Or Lessons in the Management of Love

Most of us keep dogs because they hold out the promise of uncondi-
tional love. It is their friendship, their dependence and their blind
loyalty which provides the main pleasure and motive for pet ownership. In a few dogs, this bond becomes excessive so that the dog is
insecure and panics when left alone. Owners often misunderstand this
aspect of their dog's behavior, believing that the dog has been destructive, soiled the house and made a great deal of noise out of spite or as a
"punishment" for having been left at home. As I have said elsewhere in
this book, attachment or love is the most important motive for canine
behavior. Get the love factor right and most other aspects of the
relationship between man and dog fall correctly into place.

The most common complaint about overattachment is that the dog
is destructive when alone. There may also be breakdowns in accustomed toileting habits, barking or other distress vocalizations and
attempts made to prevent the owner from leaving home. Then there
may be a host of other neurotic, attention-seeking ruses to maintain
the attention of the owner, such as yapping incessantly when the
telephone rings or interrupting conversation with visitors and activities such as watching TV or reading.

There is an interesting concentration of particular breeds, age

groups and histories of dogs with attachment problems. In our practice, we find that it is young crossbreeds, especially secondhand dogs
who have been adopted from the pound or rescue kennel, who are
most likely to panic when alone. Of purebred dogs, Labradors have
many more separation problems compared with other apparently
similar breeds such as golden retrievers, which are rarely destructive.
The common notion about mongrels and Labradors is that they are
unfailingly loyal, so a propensity to overdependence is the penalty
that their human companions may have to pay.

Most separation problems occur in dogs under the age of two and
are a symptom of their continuing juvenile dependence. Just as the
distressed young puppy finds comfort in sucking from its mother's
nipple or chewing a stick while teething, so juvenile dogs often engage
in the anxiety-reducing "displacement" activities of sucking and tearing. Finally, purebred dogs that started their lives in "puppy farms"
and were sold through dealers show the highest propensity to problems of overattachment: five times more often in a sample of ex-
puppy-farm patients at the Animal Behaviour Centre compared with
pedigree dogs purchased directly from breeders.

## GENERAL STRATEGIES

Therapy for dogs that can't bear to be alone has a high probability of
succeeding: 76 percent of our patients get better over a three-month
period. With hindsight, most of these owners found it fantastic that
they endured such inconveniences and damage, yet the solutions we
offer are simple:

> *The human–animal relationship.* Somehow, the humans in the
> dog's life have to detach themselves and show less affection to the
> dog. There is no doubting how hard this can be; for some, making
> the cure seem worse than the condition. Small things matter, such as
> not responding to every approach by the dog with conversation, a
> stroke and fondling of ears. Make such pleasures occasional rather
> than constant. Do not fulfill the dog's every demand, be it for play,
> for exit to the garden or for the opportunity to sleep on a lap during
> the evening.

*Timing of contact.* As an expression of a generally cooler relationship, one needs to devise a practical means of separating the dog from human company for frequent, short bouts of time. This may only mean closing the door behind as you move from room to room, thereby stopping the dog from being your shadow. Aim for a target of 30 percent separation of the dog from you during daytime hours, discourage him from sleeping in your bedroom and certainly do not allow him on your bed at night.

*The manner of going.* Before you leave your dog, be especially cool, even rejecting, rather than apologetic and loving. Most of us (myself included) go through a bizarre conversational sequence with our pets, telling such well-meant lies as "Be a good boy," "Guard the house" and "I won't be long." Better to be offhand, even inconsistent in the routine and preparations leading up to departure. You can really keep the dog guessing by leaving the house via a window, dressed in casual clothes, or no clothes at all! On some days, park the car away from your house since the noise of starting the car can be the very trigger that escalates problematic separation behaviors.

*Desensitize departures.* It is helpful not to leave the dog alone for longer than his or her tolerance limit. Instead, leave for short periods, then return as though you had forgotten an item such as key or handbag. Set a target of initially five mock departures for every genuine goodbye in the early stages, and as a long-term management regime aim for a variable ratio of 1:2. The theory sounds simple but the practice may be more difficult as tolerance of separation by dogs can vary from day to day.

*Bookkeeping.* Keep careful records of your dog's behavior, noting the date, time and duration of tolerated versus non-tolerated separation. Examine these like a detective and build upon small successes.

*Creature comforts.* Ensure that your dog is well-exercised, fed, watered and left with the run of the house when you are out. It can often be helpful to leave a radio playing low. Heaven for a dog is often to be found lying on your bed or smelly worn clothes, so do consider that as an option. The more "normal" and indulgent the dog's arrangements in the house while you are away, the better.

*No punishment.* Too many owners punish or scold their dog when they discover damage to the house or a complaining note from the neighbor. This is a quite disastrous response to reunion, which should always be a mutually joyous experience. Never hit the dog who has been destructive—find personal comfort by kicking a brick or ringing a phone helpline. Take it easy!

*Alternative activities.* Remember that dogs are intelligent, manipulative and above all social creatures for whom isolation is always traumatic. At least offer the enrichment of toys referred to in Chapter 10, of which the Kong and rope-floss are probably the most suitable distractions from chewing your possessions. Consider also whether or not your dog should be left alone at all. Maybe it would be better if he accompanied you to work, even stayed in the car. Best of all, leave your overattached dog in the company of a friend if you have to be away for long periods of time.

*Drugs.* Panicky dogs have dramatically accelerated heart rates, increased blood pressure, disturbances to peristaltic movements of the alimentary tract and abnormal breathing patterns. And like anxious people, anxious dogs often hyperventilate. Most of these physiological responses are mediated by adrenalin-release, the hormone- and neuro-transmitter involved in the fear response of all mammals. For many years, drugs known as beta-blockers have been used in human medicine to alleviate the worst of these physical signs, the best-known such drug being Inderal. If the animal husbandry and behavioral rearrangements outlined earlier have not resolved the problem of your overattached canine, talk to a vet about beta-blockers and other anti-anxiety drugs which can give useful relief. Of course, drugs should be seen as providing only a short-term window of opportunity for the behavioral approach, rather than as a solution in their own right.

*The medical connection.* We often find that when dogs suddenly panic when left alone after having previously tolerated separation, the cause is likely to be a medical one. I have had many such cases in elderly dogs; for instance a ten-year-old Labrador who suddenly became panicky when alone also displayed symptoms of liver failure; in another it was due to deafness; in others the cause has been arthritis, infected ears and the trauma of being attacked by another dog. So look at your pet's eyes, ears and teeth and search for signs of inflamed skin, lameness or psychological discomfort.

* * *

The individual symptoms presented by an overattached dog vary, so I will briefly describe some additional procedures and therapies for the specific signs of overattachment.

## DESTRUCTIVE DOGS

I have seen dogs that have virtually destroyed good homes and chewed up expensive cars. There comes a point when owners can bear no more, and for them a short-term avoidance strategy against further damage is justified. At its simplest and most economical a muzzle might be fitted (see page 124). However, since dogs must be supervised when wearing a muzzle, the purpose of wanting to leave them alone is defeated. Better to use a stoutly constructed indoor kennel, or if facilities allow, an outdoor shed or kennel and run. Proprietary crates are available in a range of sizes and materials from pet stores (see page 135), those made of chromium-plated wire-mesh being the most resilient. If you construct an outdoor kennel facility, you may well incur the wrath of neighbors if your dog barks when distressed.

## LONELY BARKING

Barking consumes little effort in a dog and can be sustained for days at a time. A dog's bark is horribly penetrating in a home situation and it is not possible to change its irritating quality significantly by engineering measures such as soundproofing the room. Assuming that all of the changes in relationships have been applied as outlined in earlier sections on overattached dogs, the Aboistop might be considered. On the other hand, strange smells might make the already distressed dog even more upset. The only option open to some owners of such barky dogs is to hire a pet-sitter or place their animal into daytime boarding kennels.

## ACCIDENTS WHEN ALONE

Overattached dogs are a good illustration of the dictum that the first casualty of stress is usually bowel control. A regular peristaltic surge moves down a dog's alimentary tract at intervals of one and a half to two hours, but when stressed (an overattached, lonely dog is stressed) the gastric migrating motor complex is blocked for one, or maybe two cycles. When it finally resumes, it can travel with remarkable force and quite overcomes the dog's ability to regulate normal emptying of its rectum by relaxation of the anal sphincter muscles. Imagine how wrong it would be to return and punish such a dog, but too many owners do just that.

For practical treatment, it is sensible to fast a dog if indoor excretion is a regular problem when he is left alone. Instead of feeding him prior to your departure, feed him on your return. In addition, you can remove water if he will not be left for more than five hours. Many anxious dogs drink more than they require when stressed by separation. Thoroughly clean areas that have been urinated or defecated upon, and consider slightly restricting his space by, for instance, shutting him in one room or confining him in a crate or kennel.

## VIOLENT PROTECTIVENESS

It may seem bizarre, but many forms of aggression are provoked by the dog trying to keep his master and his friends at home, fighting off the prospect of lonely separation. I think of Jamieson, a delightfully hospitable mutt recently rehomed from London's Battersea Dogs' Home who would allow all and sundry into the owner's modest house, but then keep them prisoner! On one outstanding occasion the "prisoner" was a burglar who was held in secure canine custody until Jamieson's mistress returned.

Treatment of overly possessive dogs like Jamieson usually involves the response-substitution technique, where the dog is trained to sit on a chair or mat a small distance from the door which would otherwise be guarded. Make that response one which is highly rewarding, with payoffs of play, food and whatever else turns him on. You should leave, return, leave, return on several occasions, always rewarding him for remaining on his mat. On the final occasion and before making your genuine departure, call the dog forward and pop more food through the mail slot as a symbolic goodbye.

Finally, dogs that are excessively territorial, or protective of their owner on the leash, usually exhibit several other signs of overattachment, to be tackled not so much by active punishment as by a careful and systematic shift in the pet–owner relationship. As Omar Sharif once said, "Love is fine so long as you know how to handle it!"

# 14
# Other Behavioral Problems:
## *An Alphabetical Digest*

### BARKING

Excessive and unwanted barking is a major source of friction between neighbors and the problem is, of course, entirely avoidable. First we must consider the context in which barking occurs: territorial defense, as a component of play and general excitement, during anxiety on separation from the owner (see Chapter 13), as a compulsive behavior which provides a source of pleasurable self-stimulation (see section on obsessive–compulsive disorders, page 192) or because the behavior has been inadvertently trained by payoffs from a manipulated owner. Understanding the underlying motive will naturally suggest the appropriate solution, but here are some tips that I have found useful in practice:

*Remove payoffs.* Developing the points made earlier about analysis of causation, rearrange the dog's life so that the expected payoffs no longer appear. It may be that your constant return to reassure your barking dog is the very factor that sustains the unwanted behavior. For a territorial dog, it might be the sight of people running away from the boundary of his territory; excited barking may have elicited play from people in the past. Change the rules and thereby reverse the outcome of barking.

*Punishment.* I once visited kennels that were operated by an assertive, some would say fierce dog trainer; forty-five dogs gazed with imploring eyes from behind bars, there was barely a tail-wag of greeting and they were almost entirely mute. My host pointed to the instrument of his success at maintaining this silent regime: a light whip which he merely had to show, or whack the kennel doors, to obtain the desired conformity. It was not an approach I would recommend to others and I fear for the welfare of dogs that pass through his institution. Nevertheless, he nicely illustrated the trainability of dogs' barking. In our practice, we might use the thrown tin can instead of whips, often allied to a simple hand gesture or quietly spoken command. Be careful not to reinforce unwanted barking inadvertently by shouting or reprimanding the barking dog.

*Environmental enrichment.* Very often the barking dog is also a bored dog, so it is a high priority that the dog be given an interesting lifestyle with more stimulating and exhausting activities to perform. As a poor substitute for canine and human company, offer toys.

*Aboistop.* The technology and procedure for utilizing this device is outlined in Chapter 10 (page 127) and I believe it to be the ideal approach in many cases. Certainly, the other "final options" of shock collars or surgical devocalization (see below) are unacceptable.

*Surgery.* Each country has its own bottom line so far as the ethical treatment of animals in concerned. It is commonplace for New Zealanders to have vets surgically devocalize their dogs, particularly in urban areas. In the US, Australia, the UK and most of Europe, such a procedure would cause profound disquiet among vets and others who care about animal welfare. Depending upon the site and scale of surgery, the bark of an operated dog often recovers to a garbled cough that can be almost as irritating as the original bark.

## CAR TRAVEL

If cars have brought freedom of choice and travel to people, they have also benefited dogs, giving them a chance to travel in relative luxury. Nature could never have anticipated the extraordinary distances and extension of territory made possible by the invention of the motor car. Most dogs love to travel: the panorama of sights and smells through which they effortlessly glide in the company of a loved human would be difficult to improve upon.

But cars can also bring out problems in dogs. Some get a little too excited, and I refer to these as our car-crazy canine patients. Then there are a minority of dogs who are genuinely distressed by the car, either through past unpleasant associations and traumas, more often because of motion sickness from unusual stimulation of the body's balance mechanism. In either case, the dog is not such good company in the car and is more likely to be left at home or to be kenneled than to take a ride. All parties suffer, yet the problems associated with dogs in cars are usually easily resolved.

### Car-crazy

The excited yapping or screaming of canine patients is a regular feature of our work at the Animal Behaviour Centre. We investigate such dogs personally by taking a short car journey with the long-suffering owner. I remember a Jack Russell named Bimbo, who became something worse than a demented dervish or fly in a bottle the moment his owner touched the turn signal controls. Then again, there was a vocal German shepherd nicknamed the Great Whinge, who screamed during journeys past parks or fields, yet was quiet in cities. Such dogs are nearly always worse on the outward journey from home but usually improve on the return leg. It doesn't take much detective work to appreciate that they are excited by the prospect of release for walks. Confirmation of this hypothesis comes from our finding that seven out of ten car-crazy patients rode in the car for all or most of their outings when they were young. Dogs that only occasionally go in the car or experience less stimulating journeys' ends, such as to the supermarket parking lot or the veterinary surgeon, do not become crazed in the car.

Excited travelers can arouse great amusement from outsiders. I recall driving in a crawl along a jammed highway alongside a harassed lady whose two cavalier spaniels were yapping in the back of her car, out of reach but with sufficient volume to wake up the baby. I wound down my window and gave a rapid consultation on how she might improve her situation on the journey between London and Liverpool. The learned basis to this problem is so predictable that I expect a high probability of success with the strategy outlined below, and the lady on the highway wrote a week later to say that, indeed, a miracle had been worked when she stopped at the next service station to reorganize the dogs in the car. Some or all of the following tips can be helpful in reforming the car-crazy dog:

*Change the purpose of travel.* Don't just use the car to go to exciting venues like the park with your dog. Drive to relatively boring places like indoor multi-story garages when doing the shopping, and leave the dog in the vehicle. Frequently drive the dog "nowhere" and then return home. If you have to release the dog from your car for a walk, make him wait a few minutes, thereby decreasing the excitement of arrival.

*Restrict view and movement.* If your dog is tethered low in the car where he can't see over the windowsills, he is likely to be calmer. In practical terms, the rear-seat floor is the ideal environment, lowest and closest to the car's center of gravity. From this perspective he will relate to events within the car rather than outside.

*Tether rather than confine.* Dog guards and other means of confinement to the backs of cars insulate dogs from physical contact with their owners: They are in a private world where they can do as they please. Much better to bring dogs forward, but for safety reasons they should be tethered. Mention was made on page 121 of car harnesses, which can have an admirably calming effect upon some dogs. For more vigorous dogs, tethering by the collar on a short leash or better, by a halter, stops movement and with it the opportunity to self-stimulate. The effect can be dramatic once the dog has been gently accustomed to restriction. Such confinement probably seems as strange at first to a dog as it is to humans when we first wear seat belts.

*Distraction.* In sound-sensitive dogs, an aural alarm can have a powerfully quietening effect. Unfortunately, in others it can arouse them to even noisier efforts! For those that are sound-sensitive, the

mere sight of an aerosol alarm is sufficient to interrupt unwanted
in-car hysteria. Equally, a water pistol may have the desired effect
upon a few dogs, but it is not, unfortunately, a universal cure.

*Payoffs for peace.* It is important that you structure your interactions with the dog so that calm behavior is rewarded but exuberant
behavior does not produce unintended payoffs. Too often, owners
do the latter. The most powerful punishment for undesired behavior is to stop the car. For reasons of road safety, do not perform
emergency brake-stops on a busy highway, but you may be able to
do them on a quiet boulevard or country lane. Establish a constant
criterion of acceptable peacefulness versus unacceptable noisiness;
praise the former but punish the latter. In practice, this strategy may
not be easy to apply, because dogs can be very persistent and
modern roads are too dangerous for drivers to be anything less than
100 percent attentive to their driving.

*Diversions.* The response-substitution training approach outlined
on page 52 can be used in the car, but only with a passenger
assistant to perform the training. The substitute behavior may be
"down" or "sit" and "lift a paw."

*Exhaustion.* Dogs should always be walked before car journeys. It
is lazy of us to drive our dogs routinely to open spaces and release
them direct from the backs of cars. A period of formal and controlled walking on the leash creates a positive and disciplined relationship between companions.

*The failures.* Yes, I will admit to having had failures with the above
approaches, but my failure rate has dramatically decreased since
the availability of the scent-releasing Aboistop (see page 127). In
other cases, close confinement to a small carrying-crate, which can
be covered with blankets, rather like the proverbially chirping bird
with covered cage, can work well. When owners are under pressure
from a determinedly car-crazy canine, any *ad hoc* solution can
reasonably be considered.

### The fearful traveler

The first experience of a puppy in the car often cuts the deepest
impression upon its behavior thereafter. A stressful car journey for a
puppy that vomited while being collected from the breeder is a bad

start to life. I have treated only fifteen dogs that were genuinely afraid of cars over the thirteen years of our behavioral practice at the Animal Behaviour Centre, but I am sure there are and will be more who will benefit from the strategy we successfully devised for Cluedo, a cairn terrier who hated cars. Poor Cluedo was the pet of a broken marriage who spent weekends with husband, Monday to Friday with wife. That admirable arrangement entailed an obligatory fifty-mile journey, during which Cluedo became a panting wreck, salivated over the back seats of the car and was then exhausted for the ensuing twenty-four hours. If Cluedo did not improve, there was every prospect he would not be able to make the journey. We applied most of the following techniques for Cluedo's benefit:

*Playtime in the car.* The car should be positioned in the driveway or off the road, so that ball games can take place safely in and through the stationary car. Most simply, open all doors and toss the ball from side to side. In addition, feed the dog in the car, have him sleep in it (in shade if during the summer) and generally create an image of life in a kennel-on-wheels.

*Desensitize to travel.* The process of systematic desensitization is outlined on page 185. Basically, it means a little at a time, keeping the level of stimulation below the fear-threshold. In Cluedo's case, the car could travel about half a mile before he showed the first signs of physiological arousal and salivation. Journeys in his case were specified at one hundred yards or less, to the amusement of neighbors. On return from such a brief journey, the dog must always be given an appropriate reward, be it play, roughhousing or a tidbit. Gradually increase the duration and distance, as well as the speed traveled, always remaining within the dog's personal tolerance limit.

*Drug therapy.* In Cluedo's case, as in others, hyperventilation and arousal of the sympathetic nervous system blocks conscious accommodation of the dog to his situation. Accordingly, beta-blockers can be useful in reducing the fearful dog's response to the surge of adrenaline. The rationale to using beta-blockers is explained on page 168.

*Position preferences.* Encourage the dog to travel in the center of the car, where there is least swaying and stimulation of his balance mechanism. Many dogs are at their best traveling on the front passenger seat, but be sure that position does not interfere with driving skills. Alternatively, have a passenger give assistance by holding and distracting the dog.

*Fast travelers.* If vomiting is the principal first symptom of distress in a nervous car traveler, a fast of between twelve and twenty-four hours before traveling is sensible. The benefit of this approach is to create a positive expectation of arrival at journey's end, and with it a meal or tidbit.

*The pleasures of journey's end.* The most powerful reward for tolerated journeys in dogs is usually to be released for a walk. Thus, apply the opposite strategy to that recommended for the car-crazy patient and use the car as a regular intermediary between home and the park.

Finally, dogs that are bad car travelers may just be responding to a particular car. Check it out by comparing his reactions to a voluminous family-sized car, a sporty two-seater or a van. I had a bearded collie patient who was only upset in a certain car, and the problem had begun only recently. We traced his reaction to a low-level rumble from the car's worn-out wheel bearings. When they were repaired, so also were the dog's reactions.

## COPROPHAGIA

In polite company, few of us will admit that our dogs eat feces. In fact, it is surprisingly common behavior in many carnivores, who can obtain useful nutrients from the feces of other animals. When they are young and rapidly growing they will sometimes even eat their own feces, much to the disgust of human onlookers. Remember that one of the first attractions of the wolf entering human settlements would have been to clear up our ancestors' middens. So coprophagia should not be seen as a vice, rather as a functional behavior that is part-learned and which can be modified. Coprophagic dogs certainly do not deserve a hysterical reaction from their people.

Young growing dogs have a high energy requirement, and it has been shown that they obtain useful nutrition from eating their own and other dogs' feces during this critical phase. Fortunately, after growth has been completed and with more attractive alternative food sources, feces-eating usually stops. However, a greedy Labrador or beagle is quite likely to continue to scavenge food wherever it may be found, including feces. Coprophagia may be precipitated by illness, such as during gastrointestinal disturbances where absorption of nutrients is interfered with. The animal may carry a high worm burden or be fed on an amino acid–imbalanced diet. In such conditions, it is obvious that the underlying clinical cause should be attended to—for instance, routine worming at six-monthly intervals is good practice when dealing with a coprophagic dog.

Research has shown that dogs eating their own feces do not necessarily present a health risk either to themselves or to human beings whom they may occasionally lick. The great worry is about the zoonotic transfer of the roundworm egg, Toxocara. It is reassuring to know that the Toxocara egg must first be dried after being excreted by the dog in feces, and live outside the body for some three weeks before it becomes infective to humans. Nevertheless, there is no doubt that coprophagia is an emotionally repelling activity that is probably best curbed. This is what to do:

*Meal frequency.* Since coprophagic dogs are usually also hungry dogs, it is best to spread their food rations across three or four meals per day, or even allow the dog to eat what it wants, when it wants.

*Fiber fills.* A physically full stomach gives a feeling of satiety, and high-fiber diets are therefore better than refined foods. The bulk of the diet can be modified either by selecting a complete dry diet known for its high-fiber content or, alternatively, by boosting fiber levels artificially by the addition of, for instance, scalded wheat bran, shredded paper tissue (e.g., white Kleenex), refined wood pulp or ground alfalfa meal. The addition of high-fiber garden vegetables such as cabbage or carrots all help to make the dog feel contentedly bloated.

*Training.* If the dog eats only its own feces, it is sensible to train it to defecate to a strict command, at a place which becomes inaccessible later on. Ideally, one should be a good citizen and pick up feces in one's own garden as well as in public places. Reward the dog for "going" with tidbits and praise.

*Lifestyle.* There is ample evidence that bored dogs in kennels are more likely to become coprophagic. Thus, enrich dogs' lifestyle and environment with toys, company, frequent walks, etc.

*Repellency.* A number of commercial preparations have been suggested for incorporation into the diets of coprophagic dogs that will eventually taint their feces. Some are based on sulphur-containing amino acids, but one that the writer has found useful is simply a ferrous sulphate preparation sold without prescription as an iron supplement for people. Feces become characteristically black after iron supplementation and, apparently, they are also less palatable to dogs.

*Punishment.* No amount of scolding seems to break a well-established coprophagic habit, the dog seemingly only waiting until its owner is absent before defecating and then having a private feast! To be effective, punishment must be remote and seemingly related to the feces rather than to the owner's presence. Conceivably, one could arrange a TV-surveillance system whereby the dog is interrupted on every occasion it consumes feces, but that is not an affordable solution for most of us. I have devised a system of chemically induced conditioned aversion, where the act of eating feces is associated with a sense of nausea in the patient. This is done by administering K-Zyne seconds after the dog has eaten feces, the subsequent ill-feelings being "blamed" upon the feces rather than upon the lithium. It is a complicated procedure that is only rarely used at the author's practice, usually on long-term coprophagics whose habit has become intolerable to the owner and which may therefore be life-threatening to the pet.

Coprophagia is one of those many problems that are better avoided than treated. Proper attention to a good diet for both puppy and adult, as well as an effective and caring approach to housebreaking, should prevent the unpleasant problem of coprophagia. A dog's lick can then be a source of pleasure, not of horror.

## FEARS AND PHOBIAS

In the animal world, the best defense against danger is flight, so caution toward novel situations can be a life-saving attitude. Domestication of the dog has involved a marked reduction in this tendency to mistrust novelty and we are constantly challenging our pets with situations that would have provoked fear in the ancestral wild dog.

The distinction between being adaptively cautious as opposed to disablingly fearful is a narrow one, but we all like to see our dogs confident and enjoying themselves. Several factors contribute to the overall expression of fear: genetics, early experiences, trauma, health factors and the dog's relationships with its people.

The inherited basis of fearful behavior in various breeds of dog has been demonstrated many times, and we can identify nervous strains of pointers, dalmatians, briards, German shepherds and collies, to name just a few breeds. The causes and expressions of fearfulness may be different in each case, but suffice it to say that it is vital for breeders only to select dogs that are confident and outgoing specimens of their breed. Under no circumstances should an unduly nervous dog be mated simply in the hope that the experience of motherhood might magically improve her behavior.

No matter what the cause of nervousness is in a particular dog, my advice is usually never to give up on the problem. Specific fears directed at a narrow range of events or stimuli such as toward loud noises, men in glasses or hot air balloons are referred to as phobias and will be dealt with separately from general nervousness.


### The nervous dog

There is every reason why we should pity the nervous dog: for him danger lurks at every turn, friends cannot be trusted and his whole body is tuned to flight and self-preservation. The paradox of having such a pet is that our natural human instincts to comfort the frightened can quickly backfire: We can too easily inadvertently reinforce or deepen the dog's anxiety. It may seem a harsh prescription, but put sentimentality to one side and go for the cheerful, no-nonsense approach as follows:

*Ever forward!* The act of running away is self-reinforcing, making the dog feel "better" for retreating from the stimulus of which it is afraid. Thus, it becomes important to prevent retreat, so long as there is humane treatment of the animal. For fearful behavior outdoors, the solution may be simply to have the dog wear a halter and maintain his position on an extending leash when, for instance, he is approached by a stranger.

*Reinforce tolerance.* Just a look, a touch or a soft word from the loved human in a dog's life can have a quite different effect from the same treatment coming from a stranger. Kindness from a stranger should reduce fear and evoke a combination of curiosity and reciprocal friendship. However, from the loved and familiar person, the same treatment completes a simple learning process where the physiological and behavioral expressions of fear (trembling, dilated pupils, elevated heart rate, involuntary urination and of course running away) become cued or conditioned to friendly gestures from the owner. Without the conditioned stimulus of an anxiously supportive owner, the conditioned response of fear will not occur. Simply a change of attitude to being extrovert and insufferably jolly removes these triggers to an anxiety attack.

It is well-known among the show-dog fraternity that professional handlers usually obtain a more stylish performance from a nervous dog than his loving owners. The usual explanation is that human anxieties somehow "run down the lead" to affect the dog's behavior. I have little doubt that nervous dogs do indeed usually behave better with a stranger, but my theory is that strangers don't recognize all of the subtle signs of fear in the dog, carry on regardless and so don't inadvertently reward them.

*Optimum stimulation.* One could imagine a U-shaped curve to describe a relationship where increasing levels of stimulation or novelty are first liked but then create fear. Simply put, change is good but only in moderation. With the needs of nervous dogs in mind, the priority for their rehabilitation is to stimulate them at just the right, tolerated level. We thereby exercise the dog's physiological and psychological coping mechanisms, strengthening his capacity to deal with more extreme situations.

*The long leash.* Carrying a frightened dog or keeping it on a short leash and close to us reliably worsens expressions of fear. The point was well-illustrated to me by Timmy, an apricot poodle patient of mine who was supposedly racked with pain from spinal disk problems. With his mistress, he was always anxious and pestering her to be carried, seemingly unable to walk. With me and colleagues at the Animal Behaviour Centre, Timmy walked just fine. The extending leash makes counter-conditioning against such neuroses much easier than with traditional equipment. I obliged Timmy to walk the extent of the leash, thereby creating a challenging expanse for him to cross independently of his owner.

*Partnerships.* I explained earlier how dogs mimic one another as well as their owners, and mimicry can both help and hinder therapy for the fearful dog. Determine by trial and error whether the company of another dog makes the patient more outgoing or more fearful. An outgoing dog may lead an otherwise frightened individual into a situation it would not explore on its own, but a nervous companion usually has the opposite effect. On the other hand, where one dog has a despotic, almost persecutory relationship over another, the effect is usually one of exaggerated fearfulness. Remove the despot and the personality of the suppressed dog flowers. That situation often arises when owners retain a puppy from a litter which they have bred themselves, running daughter or son alongside mother. By her continuing maternal dominance, some female dogs suppress the development of initiative-taking behaviors in their offspring. But of course, there are other mother–offspring pairs where the puppy does develop into an effective and outgoing adult.

## Phobias

Irrational fears which persist and undermine an animal's enjoyment of life are called phobias, where fear is out of all proportion to the objective dangers. In humans, the most common phobias are extreme and disabling fears of spiders, of snakes, of heights or of darkness. A few dogs also show an aversion to certain animals, such as to men wearing glasses or in uniform, but the overwhelming majority are phobias toward noises. Of these, a fear of sudden, loud noises such as thunder or gunshot account for over 80 percent of our canine phobic patients at the Animal Behaviour Centre.

In many of the dogs we see, a noise phobia can be sudden in onset, traceable to a distinct event such as a fireworks party or a gun being let off close to the dog. However, an interesting minority seem to develop their phobias by chance and we are unable to identify a single, traumatic episode. Their fears develop gradually and appear to have been learned or acquired by a systematic conditioning process. Just as a fear can be learned, so it can be unlearned and there should be reasonable prospects for behavioral therapy.

The emotional life of a dog is intimately connected with its internal physiology, particularly the connection between central nervous and endocrine systems. Once these systems have been turned on, panic rules the animal and blinds it to sensible dealings with a familiar world. The first priority for treating such dogs is to find a drug therapy that attenuates the internal physiological expressions of fear, thereby freeing the animal to attend to the world around it. These drug therapies require skilled veterinary judgment and have to be tailored to the individual dog:

*Anti-panic drugs.* Drugs are widely used for treating hypertensive and fearful human beings, but sometimes they have habit-forming or other unwanted side effects. Dogs are different from people in their responses to drugs so owners should never slip their pet Valium or Elavil simply because it was helpful to the owner when they themselves felt depressed or anxious. This is a complicated specialty of veterinary pharmacology and the search is still on for safe and more effective antianxiety drugs to treat fearful dogs.

In the author's practice, we have found that beta-blockers of the sort which are used to treat human patients with high blood pressure, or musicians, actors and students with "performance nerves," can be helpful for treating phobic dogs. Their most beneficial effect is to stop hyperventilation, the rapid, shallow breathing which can bring the dog almost to the point of unconsciousness. By slowing down heart and respiratory rate, one also controls the physical signs that precipitate psychological panic.

In addition to beta-blockers, vets sometimes utilize other sedatives or tranquilizers, including the widely prescribed diazepam and amitriptyline. Such drug therapy needs to be carefully and professionally monitored for both positive and negative developments. At the Animal Behaviour Centre, we usually prescribe beta-blockers for long-term therapy (months rather than weeks) but in the short term (the first two or three weeks) we combine it with the antianxiety drugs.

*Homeopathic preparations.* The art of homeopathy has attracted a loyal following among a small number of veterinary surgeons, who have sometimes claimed. spectacular successes in treating chronic phobias using homeopathic preparations. The principle of homeopathy is that treatment mimics symptoms of the disease, but the scientific basis of homeopathy has never been satisfactorily explained. Homeopathic medicine is an individual and skilled practice very different from the bogus remedies often described as homeopathic or herbal on sale in shops or from mail order. I have written to some of the companies marketing these potions and asked for evidence of their efficacy, but the replies were not convincing.

*Diet.* The issue of how diet affects behavior is discussed elsewhere in this book. Suffice it to say that it is a topic of immense complexity. As a matter of routine, we place our phobic canine patients on a high-quality low-protein diet, usually a rice-mutton mixture (see page 112). In some but not all cases, the response to dietary management is spectacular. Chloe was an eight-month-old bull terrier who was afraid of bright lights and reflections. She could only remain peaceful in a dark or shaded room, but became a normal, outgoing bull terrier within forty-eight hours of commencing the rice-mutton diet.

*Systematic desensitization.* This term may sound a mouthful, but the theory is simple. It is to present repeatedly some stimulus of which the animal is afraid, at a low level and paired to a pleasant outcome. For instance, with a person afraid of spiders (arachnophobia), psychiatrists may seat the person in a room that is clear of all spiders, then ask them to think about a really tiny spider. Having done so in a calm fashion, the patient is congratulated and possibly given a token reward, such as access to reading favorite comics or a pleasurable massage. From the beginning, the therapist progresses to more realistic presentations of spiders, like being in the same room as one and coming ever closer, even touching it. The theory sounds straightforward, but believe me, in relation to dogs suffering from chronic noise phobias, the practice is difficult.

With dogs, we aim to reproduce the stimulus of which the animal is afraid but attenuate it to a low intensity or brief duration so that it is not frightened. For instance, in the case of a storm phobia it would have to be a tape recording of the earliest rumbles of thunderstorms, played on the best audio equipment at low intensity. If it was a fear of gunshot, we may use tape recordings. Alternatively, an assistant can fire a cap gun or starting pistol at a distance from the patient.

Retreat or obvious signs of fear indicate that the therapist has chosen too high a sound intensity for the patient, and the volume control on the hi-fi should be turned down, or the man with the pistol made to go farther away. However, recognition of the sound without fear should be rewarded with joyful play and whatever else turns the dog on.

We have to be systematic in applying the program, working to a therapeutic plan and trying to quantify the progress of treatment over several weeks of effort. The quantification may be measured in terms of the distance between patient and the man with the gun, or settings on the volume control of the hi-fi. After three to four sessions at a given intensity, one can then go on to increase the stimulus, but always remaining within the dog's tolerance limit. If the stimulus evokes fear, return to an earlier setting at a lower intensity.

The difficulty with using this learning approach is that it is impossible to reproduce on tape all of the complex elements of a phenomenon like thunder. These are light flashes, changes in humidity, air pressure, infrasound and ultrasound, all and any of which can influence the dog's behavior. A conventional audio speaker gives a poor reproduction of a narrow element of the sound of thunder. Then again, in the real world the owner may not be present and the dog has to face thunder alone or outdoors. Systematic desensitization usually has to be conducted in the room where the hi-fi is set up and the owner present.

*Hearing attenuation.* There is little doubt that some dogs experience physical pain from loud noises, and it is fear of further pain that sustains their noise phobia. With such dogs, I have explored all manner of ways to reduce the dog's hearing sensitivity, for instance using in-dwelling foam ear protectors, external earmuffs, or playing distracting white noise from a Walkman strapped to the dog's body.

Relief for such constitutionally sound-sensitive dogs might come with old age and the onset of deafness. It is possible to reduce sound-sensitivity, or even induce deafness by surgical intervention (risky) or antibiotics. However, these latter two options raise serious ethical issues which I have, thankfully, not yet had to face; is it right to deprive a noise-phobic dog of its normal sense of hearing?

## ACCIDENTS (HOUSEBREAKING)

The dog would never have been successfully domesticated were he not so easy to housebreak. By that, I mean train to deposit urine and feces away from the central core territory and therefore away from human habitation. Yet a few individuals do not quite make the connection and owners become distressed that the dog is "dirty," "naughty" or in some other way taking its revenge. Of course, we have no evidence that these intellectual processes occur in dogs, so let us examine what can be done to simplify house-training. To a large extent, techniques for housebreaking adult dogs are an extension of those applied to puppies in the twenty-week system (see Chapter 7), but the rules will be reiterated here.

If the problem is one of leg-cocking urination in a male dog, with chemical marking of the environment as the chief motive, then a hormonal approach with a view to castration is the sensible first priority (see page 195). Here we are only dealing with undesired eliminatory behavior: deposition of urine and feces in a place that is acceptable to the dog but unacceptable to humans.

*Mealtimes.* Adjustment of the timing and composition of meals should be made so that the dog will want to go out when humans are around.

*Outdoor positive training.* Accompany the dog to places you want him to go and reward him when he performs on command.

*Indoor hygiene.* Clean areas that have been soiled by your dog, ideally with a biologically based detergent. A number of proprietary products are available from pet stores and veterinary surgeons, but a cold-wash enzyme detergent is as good as any. Make up a concentrated stock solution and sponge it on. Fatty deposits that may stain fabrics can be removed with an organic solvent. Generally speaking, do not use traditional, phenol-based disinfectants whose strong odor may mask the problem without removing the offending biological messages in urine and feces.

*Repellents.* A host of dog repellents are marketed as aerosols, powders, electrically shocking devices and the like, but in my experience most of them are flawed, some just a con. The most efficient repellent of all for defecation is to feed the dog where he should not go. Nice dogs do not eat beside their midden!

*Timing.* Some dogs forget to "ask" to leave the house to go outdoors, and in such cases the owner must take over control of their bowels and bladders. This is best done by using an oven timer, set to ring at one-hour intervals. Quite soon, a conditioned response to the oven timer will be formed: you go outside together to the allocated spot, and bingo!

*Restriction of movement.* Exercise and activity stimulate the urge to defecate, so it follows that restriction of movement might inhibit the process. In practice, that may be achieved by keeping the dog in a small room if the problem arises overnight, perhaps tying him to one's own bed if he wanders off when you are asleep. A better option is crate training (see page 135).

*Instrumental control.* Chapter 6 describes a simple method for conditioning a dog to excrete to a simple word signal such as "busy," following it with ample praise and play for each defecation and urination in the desired location. This can be particularly useful when you are in a hurry but the dog is not!

*Good citizenship.* Most urban areas have scoop laws to make people pick up after their dog; it makes sense if owners want to get along with their community. There is an immense variety of scoops and gizmos on the market, but few are more effective than a plastic bag (without holes!). Place your hand inside the bag, then using it like a glove, pick up the stools with it, folding the bag inside out and tying it up. You can dispose of it in special bins if they are provided, or take it home.

## LIVESTOCK CHASING

American scientists recently measured levels of a key amino acid (tyrosine) in the brains of dogs from breeds used for herding, and compared them with levels from breeds selected to guard. Examples of the first would be Border collies, of the latter Pyrenés or Maremmas. Remarkable differences between them were discovered, which means that there are innate or genetically determined differences in the neurochemical makeup of dogs who chase and those who just lie around. The chasing instinct is particularly high in some of the breeds of dogs that come to our practice, notably in boxers, Border collies (more than in rough collies), greyhounds and their lurcher derivatives and many terriers. Chasing can be an overwhelming compulsion for those dogs and I think they may even dream of chasing animals like chickens, squirrels, sheep or deer.

Looked at from the perspective of wildlife biology, dog owners can rationalize that their pets are somehow acting in the role of a benign Darwinian selector, increasing the "fitness" of animals whose natural predators were long ago exterminated. That view is neither humane nor practical, and I worry about the suffering imposed upon the hunted animal. That is why I have tried to find a reliable and humane method to stop dogs chasing and killing.

In the wild, hunting is a skillful process which involves trial and error and is rewarded by results. Hunting also has its penalties for failure to capture the prey, and more particularly for being injured during the chase. In a long-running survey of wolf kills upon caribou and other nimble-footed ungulates in North America, Dr. David Mech found that only a small percentage of attempted kills upon deer were successful. The remainder were aborted early on, usually when the prey detected approaching wolves and ran off. Then again, wolves learn to avoid species such as elk and musk ox, which have powerful and dangerous hooves or horns, except when they have the advantage in deep snow, boggy ground or the prey is injured. Danger is a good teacher and while hunting has its inherited components, there are also strong learned elements too. Just as a habit can be learned, so it can usually be unlearned, as I have proved again and again with livestock-chasing dogs at the Animal Behaviour Centre. Proceed as follows:

*Safety first.* Remember that all animals have rights and we must not endanger their lives for the sake of a dog. Thus, make sure your dog is wearing a muzzle if he might break free and attack, and certainly he should be restrained on a reliable collar (check for strength) with a long line of, say, fifteen feet attached, in addition to an extending leash. With these precautions, you can always run after and catch the dog if you should mistakenly drop the extending leash.

*Choose your location.* At the farm from which we operate our practice, there is a plentiful supply of all the regular farm livestock: sheep, cattle, horses, chickens, geese, goats, donkeys and more.

They are all accustomed to our antics as we circulate with cocky canines who believe that fur and feather is just for fun. Having access to such facilities is an immense advantage in our work, and the reader may well have to take up sheep-keeping or make friends with a local farmer to engage in the training programs outlined below.

*Obedience.* Perfect compliance with the usual obedience commands is required, with occasionally a degree of compulsion in the old-fashioned way. For instance, there should be no question of compromise in demanding 100 percent compliance to the "come-sit-stay" commands.

*Punishment.* A rattle tin can is by far the most effective punishment for this purpose, where it is delivered with good timing to coincide precisely with the rush forward and near-contact with the victim animal. Study the technique outlined on page 114, and be sure that you are a skillful operator before putting animals at risk.

*The victim fights back.* The ideal circumstance is to have hand-reared animals that are fearless of dogs, indeed attack-trained sheep or aggressive chickens which will deliver to the dog as good as he gives. This is the basis of the old-fashioned shepherd's method, where the hapless dog was penned among aggressive rams and frightened, even injured. Unfortunately, that technique may work on a minority of dogs, but in our experience there is a poor transfer from the sheds or corrals in which the head-butting rams are encountered to open fields where the killing tends to be done. The training environment must be realistic and as similar as possible to the real world.

*Conditioned aversion.* This technique makes the animal ill in the company of sheep and produces a powerful aversion to the smell, perhaps even to the sight of sheep. The technique was originally devised by the U.S. Wildlife Service to reduce predation upon sheep by coyotes. I have proved that dogs think somewhat like coyotes, but the method, which employs lithium chloride as the aversive agent, can be time-consuming and is strictly for skilled professionals.

*The shocker.* We have already discussed shock collars and I explained why I disapproved of their widespread use in dog training. However, they can be effective in conditioning a fear of sheep and other livestock, and it is the only application of this otherwise cruel training system that I can square with concern for animal rights. However, dog-owners should not purchase and use such equipment except under expert guidance and certainly not before trying kinder alternatives.

*Practice makes perfect.* Human instinct is usually to avoid trouble, but if you want to discourage your dog from chasing livestock he should be constantly re-exposed to that evocative stimulus. Eventually, the dog adapts or becomes bored with cats or sheep and the chase tendency is replaced by other interests, such as rolling in manure or performing object retrieves for the owner. So if a training program to stop sheep-chasing is to be effective, frequent, mass exposures to sheep walks should be planned over a short time. In our practice, the prospects of successfully treating a farmer's dog for sheep-chasing are usually higher than for suburban dogs, which only occasionally meet sheep.

*Problem avoidance.* Puppy training is the first priority for owners of all dogs, which should include contact with the various forms of livestock that will eventually be encountered in later life. It is so easy to condition a young puppy not to chase, more difficult when the habit is established.

*Security and peace of mind.* The legal and financial liabilities of having a dog that chases and kills livestock can be horrendous. I recently saw a boxer that chased a horse and dislodged its rider, who was injured in the fall. The horse went on to cause a road traffic accident in which two people were also injured. Outstanding claims for damages and legal bills are unimaginable, but fortunately my client had invested in pet insurance. Household insurance policies sometimes cover these liabilities, but it is sensible to check. Then again, if you have a dog with the slightest tendency to chase livestock, people, animals, or vehicles, invest in good fencing. There can never be peace of mind if there is a possibility of your dog escaping.

If you live in suburbia or the city, it is best just to avoid walking your dog near farm livestock or at least keep him on a leash. Finally, if you have two dogs, the probability of their going off on a hunting trip dramatically increases compared with a single dog. Dogs usually need a partner to hunt with, so reduce the risks by keeping one of a pair indoors or on an extending leash when the other is free.

## Obsessive-Compulsive Disorders

Anyone who has visited a zoo cannot have failed to notice the constant pacing, circling, licking and other repetitive behaviors exhibited by bears, giraffes, elephants and other large mammals. Even the reptiles throw themselves at the glass and engage in futile climbing efforts, then crash down and repeat the behavior without any apparent logic. We now know that these abnormal behaviors are caused by denial of the company of their own species, an abnormal and artificial environment, the wrong diet and mistimed meals and other factors. These are symptoms of extreme unhappiness, even madness in animals. That is why I find the capture and confinement of wild animals distasteful and unacceptable to a civilized society.

Unfortunately, it is not just at the zoo that we see animals behaving oddly: they are also to be found down on the farm, in laboratories and in the homes of pet-owners. In our behavior-therapy practice, the compulsive disorders of dogs are some of the most extraordinary we encounter. Though they may seem faintly amusing to the outsider, for the owners and those who live with the dog, they can be very tiresome. In the table below, I have listed the various compulsive disorders that occur in dogs:

Licking /self anointing  
Object-chewing  
Air-swallowing                    *Oral behaviors*  
Excessive drinking  

Light-chasing  
Shadow-chasing  
Fly-catching                      *Visual disturbances*  
Place fixations  

Pacing  
Jumping  
Circling                          *Movement stereotypes*  
Tail-chasing  

Self-mutilation

In our practice these sometimes disastrous problems are seen in about 5 percent of our canine caseload, and a Canadian colleague has reported an even higher frequency in the Toronto area. The common denominator of such problems is stress from attempts by animals to deal with irreconcilable conflict. They are more likely to be seen in dogs that have recently been kenneled or have changed hands; perhaps they have been subjected to undue punishment or trauma. It may be that there is a new baby in the house, a persecuting kitten, or a puppy. It can be as simple as the husband leaving home or an expression of grief. The symptoms are always dramatic and the mistake of some owners and experts is to focus unduly upon the extraordinary behavior without identifying the underlying cause.

Rocky was one such case who came to see me a year ago: a thirteen-month-old male rottweiler who for the last five weeks had been attacking shadows. It did not have to be just shadows from artificial lighting indoors; a walk outdoors on a sunny day was also guaranteed embarrassment for Rocky's owners. Rocky's nose was constantly cut and bruised from being smashed into the ground and he was becoming a tired and tiresome companion. It was found that the onset of the problem was connected with increasing aggression toward male dogs, for which Rocky's owner had sought the help and advice of the local rottweilers dog training club. Harsh corrective procedures involving a choke chain and worse were applied to Rocky, having the unfortunate side effect of making him nervous of even the sight of other dogs at training classes. Outside the classes, he remained just as aggressive to dogs he met in the park, on pavements and the like. Because of this problem, Rocky's exercise was restricted to a few minutes' walk on pavements, usually after dark when there was less risk of encountering strange dogs.

Rocky's compulsion was successfully treated by first tackling the precipitating cause: his aggression to dogs. This involved the gentle schooling technique with Halti and Flexi, surgical castration (to reduce inter-male aggression) and a more normal, free-and-easy outdoor lifestyle. In the first few days after castration Rocky wore a muzzle, to find out if he was safe to meet other dogs. His exercise was extended to three hours a day: they were to become real workouts that left him exhausted after walks. Rocky was given the activity toys of a Boomer Ball for a rationed ten minutes per hour and continuous access to a Kong. The symptoms have now virtually disappeared and

Rocky only fixates on shadows if there is tension in the family or voices are raised.

General advice for treating these behaviors is as follows:

*Avoidance.* Remove all sources of stress, conflict, confinement and unnecessary aggravation.

*Feeding.* If there is an association between unwanted behaviors and being hungry (e.g., just before mealtimes), feed several small meals each day of a bulky, high-fiber diet (see Chapter 9).

*Enrichment.* Offer play and stimulating exhaustion from the company of humans, dogs and those toys again.

*Short-term protection.* Some compulsive behaviors can be life-threatening, such as when a dog nibbles its paws to the point of bleeding and infection. You should immediately consult a vet about preventative measures which might include a muzzle, a special collar, dressings, drug therapy and possibly surgery.

*Drug therapy.* The neurochemical basis of compulsive stereotypes is now well-researched and involves an old friend of risk-taking sportsmen, workaholics and high-drive personalities: endorphins. These are narcotizing agents that have similar effects to morphine and its derivatives, and which induce a high in both man and animals. Such pleasure-seeking and compulsive behaviors usually cease when a morphine antagonist is given and that response is a useful pointer to the underlying cause of the problem. Veterinary researchers hold out the promise of developing a slow-release system of drug administration which can be used to manage these obsessive–compulsive disorders, be they in dogs, racehorses or man.

## SEX

Nymphomania, impotence, bizarre sexual orientations and the like are all part of the daily practice of animal behavior therapy, and we saw from Chapter 2 that their origins can be quite complex. The most common complaint among our dog-owning clientele is that a male dog is hypersexed, trying to mate humans, chairs and other dogs of either sex.

Testosterone is only part of the drive behind male sexual behavior, and castration or hormonal therapy does not necessarily stop all interest in sex. There are also the pleasures of companionship, of play and of physical stimulation to the back, abdomen and genital areas.

Occasionally, one sees distinctly masculine behavior in female dogs, especially when they are entering proestrus (the beginning of heat), sometimes after spaying. Again, these behaviors can be ritualized or learned, just as in male dogs. The juicy topic of misplaced or excessive sexual behavior in the dog is thus not just a subject for cartoons but is also an area of interesting scientific inquiry for which several worthwhile and promising therapeutic approaches have been devised.

The great myth about male sexual behavior in dogs is that somehow they "need" the release of being mated, masturbated or otherwise sexually stimulated. This is only a rationalization based upon human experience because the reality is that ejaculation increases sperm production which in turn also increases testosterone production, further enhancing the sex drive. Although the occasional breeder asks me about how to increase sexual performance of a male dog, most owners want their dogs to forget about sex, at least in public. While there is no single strategy for overcoming problems of hypersexuality in dogs, surgical removal of the endocrine glands that are the source of male and female hormones is the most obvious first consideration. However, there are other options too.

## Castration

As a general policy for controlling unwanted production of puppies, surgical castration of male dogs and spaying of females is the most effective policy, but there will always be some uncastrated carousing males left to carry on mating. I do believe that castration is justified if it brings benefits to the individual dog, and the following behavioral payoffs have been established about the operation:

*Reduction in roaming.* There is a dramatic decrease in the motivation of male dogs to roam in pursuit of females after they have been castrated. The scent of an estrous female dog carries for miles, and is an irresistible lure to the sexually aware male dog.

*Mounting.* Mounting has neurological as well as hormonal elements but generally it too declines, by half to three-quarters, during the first three months after castration. However, a few individuals continue to attempt to mount objects even after castration, because of learned influences.

*Urine marking.* Dogs urine-mark to define territory, possibly to attract mates and generally to advertise their presence. Very frequent urine marking, especially in environments such as a friend's house, warrants castration. However, castrated males often continue to leg cock, though a few may regress to puppylike squat urination.

*Fighting.* Uncastrated male dogs are more likely to fight than castrates and the risk of a male dog being the victim of an attack is also reliably decreased by castration.

*Disadvantages of castration.* There is usually an increase in appetite and associated gain in body weight after castration, possibly due to a decrease in the animal's metabolic rate. However, control of food intake and increased exercise should prevent this from happening.

A minority of castrated dogs seemingly become attractive for "rape" by uncastrated males. The story is an interesting one, where the acid-producing bacteria in their anal sacs change from producing the smells characteristic of an uncastrated male to those more like a sexually attractive female. The process is reliably suppressed by injection of synthetic testosterone, but more practically by introduction into the anal sacs of an antibiotic effective against anaerobic bacteria. In a few castrates, the problem of lusting dogs can be a continuous source of distress. For these, it may be best to remove their anal sacs surgically.

## Training

If jumping onto the leg of every crouched human evokes an excited scream, a dog will tend to continue performing in this way. If, however, there is a probability of an unpleasant outcome such as a mild dousing in water, time-out punishment (see page 46) or the rattle tin can, the activity is likely to diminish.

## Redirection

In uncastrated males, it may be possible for the dog's sexual behavior to be redirected away from the undesired target of his sexual fantasies to some other activity or subject. Another obliging dog may step into the role of being the sexual partner and substitute for a human. I well recall the case of a pair of dachshunds, Twiglet and Gonorrhoea, who had a lustful homosexual relationship of some fourteen years that was marked by daily half-hour sessions of anal intercourse. The arrangement was an admirable one in that it took place outdoors between consenting canines; they returned refreshed and ready for polite human company. Interestingly, Gonorrhoea eventually had to be castrated to resolve a persistent prostate gland problem, but his sexual antics were unaffected by the operation.

I have encountered many interesting and bizarre sexual attachments in dogs: toward cats, toward a duck, a particular child, a lady, the arm of a sofa, a Wellington boot, a journalist's big toe, footballs and more. Most of these are harmless, amusing and could easily be managed, redirected or interrupted.

### Impotence

It may seem surprising for readers to learn that some dogs actually do not succeed in mating a female who is apparently in the peak of estrus and behaviorally receptive. Mate selection is largely the prerogative of the bitch in wild canids, and the domestic dog is not much different except that her opportunities to choose are restricted by human interference. Subtle cues, instructions and put-off messages can be transmitted from the female to males, who will thereby be discouraged from proceeding to full coital sex. Body signals involving both movement and posture are important and there are pheromones released in saliva, urine and vaginal secretions. To a small extent, these are under voluntary control; the female can send both inhibitory and excitatory messages to her courtiers.

Occasionally, a seemingly impotent male is found to have a low rate of spermatogenesis, especially if it is from a breed or strain known to have suffered from high levels of inbreeding. My advice to owners of such dogs intended for use as studs is to allow them to engage in another activity rather than the mating game. If a male dog, no matter how fine a specimen, does not wish to engage in sex, that is obviously just what the gods intended.

## To Whom Can You Turn for Help?

The provision of advice and therapy to overcome behavioral problems in pets is a relatively recent development in an area that has traditionally been the domain of trainers. We now know that there is often a medical aspect to unwanted and abnormal behaviors in animals, which makes veterinary surgeons the more appropriate choice for a consultation about behavior. There is no single, authoritative professional body regulating the activities of dog trainers, and many who claim to be behaviorists, consultants and the like do not have any formal academic qualifications. Be warned: some can do more damage than good to your animal. My advice is always to take your problematic pet to a vet, because they are equipped to make the overall diagnosis and to deliver ethical treatment. Complicated or puzzling cases will then be referred to a specialist, perhaps at one of the university veterinary schools or to a place like the Animal Behaviour Centre.

The causes of bizarre behavior are many and complex, and owners should never feel that they are failures because they have an eccentric dog. Most of my clients turn out to be caring, responsible people who are psychologically quite normal. They had previously owned dogs without any problems at all, but then along came a canine challenge that was just too big for them to handle. Take comfort from the certain knowledge that there is bound to be someone with a dog worse than yours!

# RESOURCES

USEFUL ADDRESSES

*Animal Behaviour Centre*, P.O. Box 23, Chertsey, Surrey KT16 0PU. *Tel: 0932 566696 Fax: 0932 565979*

*American Kennel Club, Inc. (AKC)*, 51 Madison Ave., New York, NY 10010. *(212) 696-8200*

*United Kennel Club (UKC)*, 100 E. Kilgore Road, Kalamazoo, MI 49001. *(616) 343-9020*

*The Delta Society (Resource for Human/Animal Interactions)*, 321 Burnett Ave. South, Renton, WA 98055. *(206) 226-7357*

*National Association of Dog Obedience Instructors (NADOI)*, 2286 East Steel Road, St. Johns, MI 48879. *Send SASE for information*

*Therapy Dogs International*, 1536 Morris Place, Hillside, NJ 07205

*National Animal Interest Alliance*, P.O. Box 66579, Portland, OR 97290

*National Dog Registry (Tattoo registry)*, P.O. Box 116, Woodstock, NY 12498. *(914) 679-BELL*

*Morris Animal Foundation*, 45 Inverness Dr. East, Englewood, CO 80112. *(303) 790-2345*

*ASPCA*, 424 East 92nd St., New York, NY 10128. *(212) 876-7700*

FOR FURTHER READING

Budiansky, Stephen. *Covenant of the Wild: Why Dogs Chose Domestication.* New York: William Morrow & Co., Inc., 1922.

Bulanda, Susan. *Canine Source Book.* Wilsonville, OR: Doral Publishing, 1992.

Carlson, Delbert G., DVM, and James M. Giffin, MD. *Dog Owner's Home Veterinary Handbook.* New York: Howell Book House, 1993.

Fogle, Bruce. *The Dog's Mind.* New York: Howell Book House, 1990.

McLennan, Bardi. *Dogs and Kids: Parenting Tips.* New York: Howell Book House, 1993.

# INDEX

## A

Aboistop, 48, 127, 173, 176
Adopting dogs
  from advertisements, 94
  breed rescue clubs, 92–93
  bringing home, 96–97
  guidelines for selecting, 91–92
  inheriting animals, 93
  questions to ask about, 94–96
  rescue kennels/organizations, 90–91
  retired show dogs, 93–94
  strays, 89–90
  from veterinarians, 94
Aerosol alarms, 127–28
Age
  for adopting dogs, 27–28
  when taken from breeders, 26–27
Aggression
  competitive dogs and, 154–56
  dental work to control, 156
  fearful dogs and, 157–58
  hormonal therapy, 155, 161, 163
  possessive dogs and, 156–57
  preventing, 158
  sibling rivalry, 162–64
  toward other dogs, 160–62
  toward owner and family, 153–58
  toward visitors/strangers, 158–60
  violent protectiveness, 170–71
Agility, 147
Akitas, 23
Amitriptyline, 184
Animal Behaviour Centre, 17
Animals, introduction to puppies, 81
Attachment problems, 165
  destructive dogs, 169
  general strategies for handling, 166–69
  lonely barking, 169
  loss of bowel/bladder control, 170
  violent protectiveness, 170–71
Attentive line, 146

## B

Balls, 130–31
Barking
  anti-barking collars, 126–27, 128
  how to control, 66–67, 127, 128, 172–73